Perfect Lives...
...and Other Fairy Tales

What to Do When the Pursuit of Happiness is Making You Miserable

---

52 Simple Steps to Creating a Life You Love

Hunter Phoenix

CreatePub
PRESS

ARIZONA, USA

Written by Hunter Phoenix
1 Yonge St. Suite 1801, Toronto, On Canada M5E 1W7
www.HunterPhoenixCoaching.com
866-820-8585

ISBN: 978-0-9917563-1-5

Book design and text composition by Angela Basil

*This is with much gratitude to all of my wonderful clients
who have allowed me to play a small part in their lives and help them
on their journey while also furthering mine.
It's especially for Linda (my Mom), Lan (my brother) & Maria (my dearest
friend); the three people who have stuck by me through everything, with
unconditional love and friendship.*

Acknowledgments

Writing a book has been a long time dream and desire. It's something I started a few times in the six or so years before birthing this one. Every time I outlined content, then changed the title, scrapped it all and started again. Like life, the process is never perfect. It can be messy, overwhelming, steeped in uncertainty, but ultimately incredibly satisfying, humbling and revealing.

Many sections of this book were written with someone specific in mind; a friend, family member, colleague or most often a particular client. But ultimately everything here is something I felt "had to be said". It was carefully chosen to share with you; my valued reader. My intention was to create an experience for you; one that would answer your questions, motivate and inspire you to action, and gently pull you forward.

But this is in large part possible only due to the guidance and assistance I've received from others over the years that has furthered my own growth and pulled me through dark places. I want to share these people with you as I thank them for the contribution they made to my life.

Mrs. Sylvia Fox, my twelfth grade teacher. (yes, really) She was the first person in my life to really demonstrate to me what a confident, successful and accomplished woman looked like and was capable of. She nurtured my talents, and showed an unwavering faith in my capabilities; far more than I myself possessed at the time. All these years later I continue to hold her as a role model knowing that without that early help I wouldn't be writing this now.

Dr. Lynne McRoberts and "Sister" Mary MacDonald; two remarkably powerful healers. Thank you both for your years of guidance, support, and the occasional much needed little shove, and of course lending your incredible talents. You both went well above and beyond what is normally expected in those roles. You kept me moving through the scary places and taking control of my life. None of this would be possible without deep inner-work and healing that took place in the years before.

Miranda Dockstader, my publisher who is quickly becoming a business partner and a friend - thank you for coming into my life when you did and giving me the means and support to finally get this project off the ground. I'm looking forward to creating more wonderful books together!

Linda Henry, my amazing mother - and as it turns out proof reader extraordinaire. You caught the mistakes and typos that others missed... many times. Thank you for making me look good!

And to you my wonderful readers, thank you for buying this book. Ultimately, you're who it's for, and the ones who make it all possible.

Contents

Introduction

"I absolutely believe that people, unless coached, never reach their maximum capabilities."
Bob Nardelli, former CEO of Home Depot

This book isn't about being, doing and having it all.
It's about You living YOUR best life. It's about you doing what lights you up, what brings you joy and feeds your soul. No matter how far off course life has gotten, or how old or young you are.
It's not about 'no pain no gain'
or grueling boot camps.
It's also not a get rich quick scheme,
miracle diet or instant cure.

"Perfect Lives & Other Fairy Tales" is the remedy to being overwhelmed and under-satisfied. With simple, practical and do-able advice, it gives small actions that produce big results. You can follow through the program step-by-step, or jump-in and pick-up with where and what you need the most right now.

Everything in the book has been tried, tested and proven. It was born out of my own personal struggles to find happiness, success and fulfillment, combined with the desire to provide creative, **easy solutions for clients, that worked with their life choices;** not as someone else's idea of what their life should be or look like.
The basis for the book has been my own coach training + hundreds of coaching hours, and happy clients. I'm thrilled to share the simple solutions that have transformed my life and the lives of people who have allowed me to be part of theirs.

With Much Love & Success,
Hunter

"Doing the best at this moment puts you in the best place for the next moment."
- Oprah Winfrey

Part I
Laying the Foundation

The Beginning: Facing the Truth

"No one is coming to save you."

Many years ago, I remember when one of my first coaches first said that to me. I was mortified, shocked, deeply disappointed, and at the same time embarrassed to admit to both her and myself that I had secretly been hoping for exactly that.

How could she know that this was my private back-up plan? In retrospect that was easy. All anyone had to do was take a look at my life. I continually said that I wanted my life to change, and in my defense, genuinely longed for it to be so. But in actual fact I was doing very little to further the process.

I *did* want my life to change, but I didn't want to be involved in the undertaking of it. I wanted *my life* to change – my partner, my career, my finances, my dress size etc.; but *I* certainly didn't want to change.

What was wrong with me just the way I was? Was I not good enough? Lovable enough? Smart enough? Why should I change, when there was clearly so much wrong with everyone and everything around me?

As you can imagine, stubbornly holding on to that idea, kept me stuck in a repeating cycle of pain, disappointment and despair for years. I repeated the same old patterns, continually hoping for a different result. On the outside, I seemed to be fluid, adaptable and never standing still. I changed jobs, cities, countries, hair color, partners and many external things, but I kept producing the same heartbreaking results.

I had become a master of deception, both to the outside world and to myself. I clearly wanted to change, and was comfortable with it on many levels, but the core beliefs, desires and unmet needs kept me firmly rooted in place.
For me, it took a full blown life-crisis for the big changes; the important ones to begin to take hold. I was hospitalized with a life threatening condition, and not expected to live.
I had moved to a city where I had no family, no friends, and the job I moved for disintegrated. The one person (my agent) that I knew in town abruptly quit the business and left the country. And the combination with a new house and mortgage left my finances strained to the limits.

Everything in my life as I had known it was whisked away almost before my eyes. The career choices I had made weren't viable in this new city.
Barely 100 pounds, my body was weak and frail and would no longer do all of the things I wanted it to, and had become accustomed to for years.
External resources of all kinds vanished, and what I was left to draw on was myself.
The process was confusing, emotionally painful, and slow. But what other choice was there? Life gives us a sign, then a warning, then a full blown crisis. I urge you from the deepest part of my heart to take on the scary changes before they hit the crisis level.

Since then, with much patience, tenacity and self-love, I have become a master of change, and every day I witness the miraculous unfolding of a life I truly love.
Today it's my pleasure to share with you some of the processes that have helped me on this incredible journey. No

one should have to go it alone, and learning from your mistakes can be a long and unhappy road.

You certainly learn what *not* to do, but what *to* do isn't always so apparent. I believe that we're all here to help each other; to make this thing called "life" a little easier.

"It's never too late to live happily ever after."

- coffee cup wisdom

1. The Willingness to Change

"Expecting the world to treat you fairly because you are a good person is like expecting the bull not to charge you because you are a vegetarian."

Rabbi Harold Kushner, "When All You've Ever Wanted Isn't Enough,"

Paraphrasing Rabbi Mordechai Kaplan

The Beginning: "I Am Willing to Change"

The first step to changing your life is a willingness to change YOU; a willingness to let go of old habits, behaviors and beliefs, and allow yourself to be changed in the process.
No, there is nothing fundamentally wrong with who you are; but if you're unhappy, frustrated or prone to feelings of depression, something's got to give. And in my experience, even with a lot of pushing and shoving, it's seldom the outside world.

You must be willing to quiet the desperate voice of your ego, (**E**dging **G**reatness **O**ut) that tells you that you are "right" and "good" and "things should be different."
That's a comfortable little trap that you can spend years reinforcing that will never produce the results, or the feeling you deeply desire to experience.
Be willing to accept that even if you are "right" and "a good

person", and while there is some satisfaction in knowing or believing this, it's still not getting you what you want. Clinging to old ideas, hoping the world is going to suddenly conform and come around to your way of seeing and doing things, is a sure path to continued suffering and ongoing pain. So are you willing to change?

Coaching Exercise:

Take a few minutes and answer these questions as honestly as you can.

Write down your 3 Biggest Challenges in life right now.

Are you willing to be wrong about what you are currently doing in these areas?

Are you willing to be wrong about your thoughts and beliefs around these subjects?

If yes, just notice it. If no, why not?

Tip - Try completing this sentence: Being wrong about_____ would

mean_____.

What do you most want to be right about? Why?

You'll probably want to keep a journal or notebook as you work through this book and the exercises in it. Jot down your answers, and refer back to them in the weeks and months to come and just notice, what, if anything has shifted. If you're a little more of a private person and feel compelled to tear the pages up afterwards, that's fine too. But at least get them out on paper... it makes it more real! And it's always better out than in!

Affirmation:

"I am willing to change. I am willing to learn a new way of experiencing life."

2. Taking Responsibility

"Action springs not from thought, but from a readiness for responsibility."

- Dietrich Bonhoeffer

I know, responsibility isn't the most fun word. And on some level, this would all seem so much easier if it was just someone else's fault. We love to blame the economy, our parents, our upbringing, our environments, our spouses, the current government, and the list goes on.

And yes, undoubtedly, all of these things factor in and influence the overall picture of our life as we know it. But the danger lies in becoming trapped in our own stories, and the events of our past. For as many sad stories of misfortune, tragedy, abuse, and neglect that are out there, we can also find triumphs, victories and overcoming obstacles.

This is not a Pollyanna-ish pep talk or a call to "awaken the giant within". It's simply a gentle, realistic reminder, that even if you feel like you can't change a lot of things, you CAN change SOMETHING.

You're probably familiar with the saying *"a journey of a thousand miles begins with a single step"*. It's responsibility, and a little bit of faith and courage, that precedes that initial step. If you are committed to an easier, happier, richer more fulfilling life, the next step is taking responsibility for the one you've got, as well as the one you're intent on creating.

Responsibility is just that; the ability to respond. It's not blame, it's not beating yourself up for what you could or should have done differently. It's simply acknowledging that you have a part in the way things are playing out. Maybe not one hundred percent control, but yes a big part.

Most of us don't want to hear that our lives and relationships are what they are because of our own thoughts, actions, and many times, just plain stubbornness or crippling fear.
We prefer to blame our boss, our parents, our spouses etc.
We cling to a vision of the world that fully supports us in staying stuck and playing small. We can't control where we were born, to whom, what gender or race we are, but we can at least make the very best with what we've got.
And let's be honest, if you live in a country and a culture where you can afford the luxury of both the time and money to read this book (or any book!) you've already started with an awful lot!

When faced with hardship or crisis, it is normal to go through anger and a victim stage. This is when we think, "If only *'they'* wouldn't do that, and would do this instead, everything would be okay." Or "If only *that* hadn't happened, I would be so far ahead."

We can't prevent every crisis from happening, or control the actions of others. And let's face it; do you really want someone else trying to control you? What we *can* do, is to choose how we are going to deal with whatever is. Doing anything else is giving your power over to external circumstances. Waiting and hoping for the world or someone else to change, builds up false hopes. These tend to come crashing down in despair when it or they doesn't change, and won't. And all you're left with is feeling stuck and suffering.

But if you change the way you interact with the world or anyone in it, life will change the way it responds to you; it has to. Sometimes the changes will be in the direction that you want, and sometimes not. And sometimes you'll get the results you want, and sometimes not. But knowing that you have the power to affect change creates a confidence and inner strength that nothing else does.

It enables you to step out of victim mode and the suffering that goes with it, and begin to shape and direct your own life. When you begin to take at least a little responsibility for the failures and the pitfalls in your life, you suddenly have the power to begin to change it. You can then also fully own each and every triumph. If your hardships are somebody or something else's doing, then so are your successes. You simply can't blame the world for your defeats and still claim the victories.

Coaching Exercise:

Take an inventory of your life.

Look at any areas that you'd like to change. What is causing you frustration, anger, grief or fear?

Are you willing to take responsibility for this? Even if someone else is involved?

Are you willing to be 100% responsible for your own well-being?

Now, make a list of all your successes. Write down everything that you are proud of. Would you be willing to let someone else take responsibility for those?

When you give up your power in one area, you also lose it in another. See if you can allow yourself to take 100% responsibility for your life - all of it, even for a week or a day. Notice how it feels...?

Affirmation:

"I'm responsible for this."

3. Easy Steps for Lasting Results

"We all have BIG CHANGES in our lives that are more or less a second chance."
*- **Harrison Ford***

So far we've tackled the tough stuff first; facing the truth, willingness, and responsibility. On an emotional level, this can be the most challenging part of the process. The inability to not just face, but embrace these key components, keeps countless numbers of people suffering and struggling year after year. Believe me, if that's all you get out of this book, you're already well on your way.

Now that we have the groundwork in place, I'd like to offer you some simple steps to help make the changes in your life smoother, easier, more fun, and yes, permanent.

Almost everyone at one time or another has gone on a crash diet, or you at least know someone who has. They're able to shed a few pounds fast only to watch them creep back on and bring some friends with them. That's not what we're going for here.

This is in essence a life makeover, and when done gracefully, change evolves. As we allow ourselves to grow into it, we transform our lives into what we had dreamed of it being. Transformation and evolution are both simple and profound, as well as having a way of continuing on their own. This is in stark contrast to radical shifts that leave us feeling uncomfortable, awkward and longing to return to familiar turf. What follows below are some simple steps or "ground rules" for lasting, easy and positive change.

1. One thing at a time. Whenever possible, initiate change in only one area of your life at a time. Taking on too much is a quick road to overwhelm. This can lead to frustration, and the urge to retreat and look for more solid footing or safer ground. I'm not saying don't change everything, but just not today! Pick one key area and begin moving forward. This leads us right into the next rule…

2. Start small. I've read a number of books and heard many coaches say to pick "the one big thing" that's going to change your life, or move you forward the most and start with that. In my experience that is a recipe for disaster.

Your life is the way it is now because of a series of steps and a series of choices, not usually one cataclysmic event that creates our current reality. Trying to take on the "big issue" may require a lot of subtle changes in your life; it can be involved, overwhelming and steeped in fear. That's exactly why it's a big issue. It may also require a greater amount of time and patience to see results.

Is there something small you can start with? Something that is going to give you some "immediate" gratification and instant results? This will also build your confidence, your energy and help strengthen that change muscle. Getting one issue out of the way will give you the peace of mind and space to navigate other changes more easily.

3. No sudden moves or big gestures. When changing any area of your life, begin by making the most minimal change necessary to move you *towards* your goal. This is not a race and you don't have to sprint there today. Break big changes down into a series of small steps that you can implement one at a time. After you've mastered that, take the next step.

For example, if finances are an issue, start by getting really clear on your income and your expenses, then decide how to proceed. Don't cut up all of your credit cards, hire a new accountant and changes jobs all in the same week!

4. Plan. Plan. Plan. New situations, combined with uncertainty or pressure can lead us into reactive thinking, poor decision making and ultimately cause us to revert to old behavior patterns. Take changes slowly and diligently, plan for the worst; it will give you a little security and structure if things really go wrong, or just don't work out as you had hoped. It will also allow you to approach any problems with a clear mind and cool head.

5. Stay flexible. Dwight D. Eisenhower once said "Plans are useless, but planning is invaluable." I know I just said to plan, and yes, absolutely! But it's also important to remain flexible, and *expect* that things will change. Even when making the most careful plans, it's almost impossible to know every variable - and who would want to?! How boring would life be then? Things will come up, situations will change and life will just happen. Keep your eye on the prize, but role with the punches when you need to!

6. Be good to you. So much has been said about "sucking it up" and "no pain, no gain". I'm not going to lie to you; changing your life will take effort, commitment, responsibility and a little enthusiasm helps, but there is no need to suffer in the process. That actually kind of defeats the purpose. You simply can't feel bad enough to make yourself feel good. Take extra good care of yourself right now. Even positive change can come with its own stress. So be sure to get plenty of rest, eat well, exercise regularly, and show yourself more than the normal amount of understanding, kindness, compassion and self-care.

7. Timing is everything. Creativity can't grow from stress, and it's hard to create something really great when we're anxious or pressured. Whenever possible, time your changes when there is a natural lull in life. Holiday seasons or other busy times of the year are packed full enough with activities and chaos. Additional strain can easily push patience to the limits, and make your changes more difficult than they need to be. Unless it's something that demands immediate attention, waiting until you have some breathing room will give you the surest shot at success.

8. Stick to a routine. When things are changing it is important to stay connected to that part of your life that remains *unchanged.* This will help nurture feelings of stability, calm and overall well-being. Whatever healthy or positive routines you may have, stick with them, and gradually introduce new behaviors one at a time. This will also allow you to integrate the new components into your life smoothly and effortlessly. After all, the whole point of this is for life to feel good!

9. No turning back. Once you have initiated a change in your life, follow through. Backing out and starting over again can quickly breed feelings of struggle and defeat. Starting and stopping also sends the message to our unconscious that we are unreliable, making it harder for us to have faith in ourselves, our willpower and our judgment. If what you are trying to do seems like a huge challenge, chunk it down a bit until you're reasonably sure you'll be able to stick with it.

10. Look for support. More than ever, this will be a time in your life where you're going to want to have ongoing, steady support, and maybe even guidance and advice. Of course coaches and counselors are ideal for this, but if that's not possible at this time, then consider an accountability partner, or even connect more with friends. You might also want to consider classes or workshops. There is an incredible power in numbers, and huge benefits to be had from surrounding yourself with people who have a common or similar goal.

Change doesn't have to be terrifying. It can ultimately be exhilarating and invigorating. And as the old saying goes. "the only thing constant in life is change." .... so you might as well embrace it and get really good at it.

As you become a master of change in your own life, you'll find that you also inspire others to do the same in theirs. And growing and changing together can only make this world a better place.

Affirmation:

"It's only change. I'm safe!"

4. Clearing Up Loose Ends

"It is the loose ends with which
men hang themselves."
- Zelda Fitzgerald
(Wife of F. Scott Fitzgerald)

Whenever I start to work with new clients, one of the first things we do is to clean up loose ends. These are little things left undone; stray sticky notes on the desk, unpaid bills or parking fines, files that need to be sorted, correspondences that need to be returned, and just generally stuff that needs to get done before we can move forward.

Often times these can be *amazing* projects that we've begun, but at some point into them, they have begun to smell a lot like hard work, have lost their joy and their luster, and have since fallen by the wayside.

In the last month, in the midst of a major move, and even more upheaval, I became acutely aware of all of my own loose ends. Generally I'm meticulously organized, and very good at keeping things caught-up and up to date - or so I thought! But in the last 4 weeks, I was humbled and reminded of my own humanness as I struggled to wade through what seemed like never-ending mounds of boxes, papers, emails and phone calls.

"Loose-Ends" which in my office also go by the name of "Energy Drains" are just that. They sit on our desks, in our garages and inboxes, quietly nagging us, reminding us that they *need* to be done. They rob us of our creative energy and of our focus, and make it just about impossible to effectively move forward with what lights up and fulfills our dreams! Before beginning yet another new project, or embarking on a new phase in life, what better time to clean up all of your loose ends? This simple process can not only bring you peace of mind, but also create a fresh, clean space for the next great adventure or incarnation of yourself to begin!

To help you identify some of your own Energy Drains, I've included a check-list below.

Relationships

__There are people in my life who continuously drain my energy.

__I have unreturned phone calls, e-mails or letters that need to be handled.

__There is a relationship I need to deal with.

__There is a phone call that I dread making, and it causes me stress and anxiety.

Environment

__My car is in need of cleaning and/or repair.

__I have appliances that need repair or upgrading.

__My closets and/or basement are cluttered and need to be cleaned.

__Repairs need to be done around my home or apartment.

__My home is cluttered and disorganized.

Body & Health

__It's been too long since I've been to the dentist.

__I do not get the sleep I need to feel fully rested.

__I'd like to exercise regularly but never seem to find enough time.

__I have a health concern for which I've avoided getting help, or need a routine check-up.

Work

__My office is disorganized, my desk is a mess, and I have trouble finding what I need.

__My schedule is out of control and I'm always late or behind.

__I know I need to delegate specific tasks but am unable to.

__With e-mail, voicemail, and snail mail, I'm on information overload!

Money

__I pay my bills late.

__I do not have a regular savings plan.

__I do not have adequate insurance coverage.

__I have debt that needs to be paid off.

Coaching Exercise:

Looking at the list above, what loose ends do you need to clean up? Do those things that you have been dreading, putting off or simply ignoring and notice the feeling of relief you get once they are done. You'll then be ready to fully move on to the next step... and be glad you did!

If you'd like a printable version of this, be sure to visit the

Book Bonus Web Page *at the back of this book. You can download a PDF version of this list to print out and use on your own.*

5. Living Without Limits

"It's impossible, but it has possibilities."
- **Walt Disney**

Wherever we are at in life right now, is a clear indication of the limits of our own thinking. Henry Ford once said, "Whether you believe you can do a thing or not, you are right."

Surely you know people who earn more money than you do, have better relationships, better careers and seemingly better lives, yet they don't possess any special super-powers, and maybe not even your knowledge, education, skills, talent, charisma, what-have-you. So what's the difference? They have simply decided to accept nothing less. They have a bigger and broader definition of their own limits and their own life.

You are not limited to the life you have right now. In case you have any doubts, let's get clear on that. At any time we can challenge our thoughts and ideas about our own limitations. We can look a little closer, dream a little bigger, act a little broader, stretch a little farther, and form new ideas about what our own personal best is.

I love the story of the early beginnings of the famed mathematician, **George Dantzig**. George was a mathematics graduate student at the University of California at Berkley. Arriving late to class one morning George quickly copied two mathematical problems from the blackboard, assuming they were homework. When he sat down to work on them that evening, he found them the most difficult problems the professor had ever assigned. He didn't have much luck in solving them, but kept at them for days.

Finally, he had a breakthrough, solved both of the problems and took them to class. The professor told him to add his homework to a stack of cluttered papers on the desk. Reluctantly, George did.

Six weeks later, on a Sunday morning, George and his wife were awakened at 6 a.m. by his excited professor banging on the door. "George! George! You solved them!" the professor was shouting. "Yes. Wasn't I suppose to?" he answered. Since George had been late for class, he hadn't heard the professor announce that the two equations on the board were unsolvable mathematical mind teasers that even Einstein hadn't been able to answer. But George Dantzig, working without any thoughts of limitation, had solved not one, but both of problems and in only a few days. "If someone had told me that they were two famous unsolved problems, I wouldn't even have tried." George later said. Simply put, George solved the problems because he didn't know he couldn't.

Most of us have been given hundreds of reasons why we can't be, do or have something. These are bestowed upon us like crippling little gifts, neatly delivered by caring friends and family who want to keep us safe, or, unknowingly, sometimes just keep us close to them. But always bear in mind that they are usually speaking from their own perspective and their own self-imposed limitations; not from the place of your strength, your abilities, your vision or commitment.
Seldom do we even realize what we are capable of until we have actually done it - or at least come close. Until then, we

can be tempted to dwell in the shadow of doubt, believing it's far safer not to try than to risk failure and rejection. But there is no safety in stagnation. There is no safety, or comfort in denying our own abilities and relinquishing the chance to grow, develop new skills and thrive!

You see, when we challenge the limits of our abilities, we automatically expand them. We may not reach our target the first time around, but with patience, practice and perseverance, most goals will yield. Think of a professional athlete; can you imagine them quitting after their first practice or their first game? Or even their tenth? Of course not! It's a given that there are going to be hundreds of practices and hundreds of games before they reach the top tier of success. The difference is, they count every small success along the way.

So what is it that you want and have probably been struggling with? What do you wish for, but feel that you can't be, do or have? Are the limits real? Or do they belong to your parents, spouse or best friend? Do you know 100% for sure that you can't do this? Or are you basing your immobility on fear or past disappointments?

Coaching Exercise:

Take 5 minutes to complete this exercise. Answer the questions as quickly as you can. This will give you a more intuitive and real "hit".

Look at an area of your life where you feel stuck, unhappy, unsatisfied, or are absolutely longing for more. Write it down at the top of a page.

What are your thoughts and ideas about this?
Where did they come from?
Are they still valid today?
Do you know that for sure?
Did you ever test these ideas?
Were they ever valid?
What has changed since you last tried this? Have you?
What could you change?
What could you do, if you were to try to expand in this area just a little more?

What would happen if you were to treat those areas of your life like George Dantzig did with the math problems, and just sit down and begin to solve them?

Affirmation:
"I trust myself to go beyond the limits of my current environment."

6. Dealing With Distraction

"There is nothing so fatal to character as half finished tasks."
- **David Lloyd George**

Life these days seems to be moving faster than ever. Some people blame it on the internet, others on television and the media, and others still on the break-neck pace that so many of us in the Western world seem to keep.
In 2005 when I first started coaching people in significant numbers, I noticed that more than half of the people that came to me for coaching were taking anti-depressants. Today, in 2012, at the time of this writing, I personally see far fewer people on anti-depressants, (almost none) but that number has been replaced by people being medicated for ADD.
Most of us have at least a touch of Attention Deficit; short attention span, restlessness, impulsiveness, hyper focused in some moments, and easily distracted in others. We tend to get bored quickly, seek constant stimulation, and expect almost everything *NOW!*

Last week I was leading a workshop and overheard one of my students joking about a web page taking 4 seconds to load - yes, seconds. *"4 seconds!"* he exclaimed, *"Who has that kind of time!"*
Although this may have been a joke in the moment, it's all too common and unfortunately true. Internet usage statistics show us that on average, we spend less than 9 seconds on the homepage of a website we're browsing, and under a minute

on the site in total. (And just think of all the hours that go into creating that content!)

As technology increases, our attention spans are decreasing. We can move from one web page or TV channel to another more quickly than ever before. More content is available to us, and it's there 24/7, and *fast!*

The average person has between 5-7 open, unfinished projects underway at any given time. Leaving things un-done leads to feelings of overwhelm and an overall dissatisfaction. Is it any wonder that a typical symptom of ADD is a history of feeling of *"not living up to one's potential"?*

So what do we do about this? In our 24/7 lit up wired world, how do we deal with distraction? The ability to focus your attention on a specific task is crucial for the achievement of any goal and the confidence and gratification that goes with it.

First, start by getting honest with yourself. Do you generally find it tough to concentrate on things, especially work related tasks? (I've already gotten up from my desk 4 times while writing this section!)

If you're similar, consider implementing the following strategies - ONE AT A TIME.

Look into modifying your diet. High carbs, sugars, dairy and gluten consumption have been linked to attention deficit. Of course, check with your doctor or nutritionist first, and then begin cutting back on these items and see what changes.

Unplug. You don't have to be wired in 24 hours per day. Make a conscious effort to spend 30-60 minutes a day away from your electronic devices - ipads, computers, TV's and yes, smart phones. Bump this up to half a day on weekends and notice the release as you start to wind down.

Get adequate sleep. Sleep is vital for attention and focus, (not to mention restoration, revitalization and repair). Allow yourself adequate time to sleep at night, not trying to "squeeze in" an extra hour of work after midnight when you know that you have to be up at 6 am. Your bedroom should be a sanctuary; somewhere peaceful to retreat to, and free of electronics. Create a dark, quite, space that you look forward to retiring to at night, and is peaceful to wake-up to in the morning.

Lay off the stimulants. Really? Do I need to say this? As if caffeine wasn't bad enough, then there are the "energy drinks"; all of the buzz without the annoying and time consuming fluid consumption to go with it. If you catch yourself grabbing for one of these (or a double espresso) around 3pm, revisit points 1-3.

Burn the calories, not the midnight oil. Studies have shown that concentration improves dramatically after a little vigorous exercise. Regular exercise, (check with your doctor first) especially cardio, literally burns off some of that excess mental energy allowing you to focus more easily and clearly.

Monitor Your Email & Browsing Time. One of the challenges today around productivity, is that the very thing that many of us use to do our work on, can also be used to hunt for recipes, watch videos, view pictures of friends (and their cats if you're on Facebook!) check the news or the latest stock prices, shop for just about anything, or converse with modern-day pen pals (Twitter). Keep an eye on the time when you open your email or browser window. Limit it to 15 minutes at a time during precious work hours.

Add a little fun! We all concentrate better on things we find enjoyable! If you're having a tough time focusing in on tasks at hand try incorporating more rewards and more breaks. Allow yourself that 20 minutes of video gaming, or Facebook-ing, channel or internet surfing, but only after you've reached a marker point in your work.

Coaching Exercise: This is not a complete list, but if you're in the "attention challenged crowd" you're probably starting to get bored already. Try implementing the above steps over the next couple of weeks, and notice if you find just a little more calm and ease.

Affirmation:
"There is exactly enough time to do everything that needs to get done."

7. Take Time For Your Life

"Well done is better than well said."
- Benjamin Franklin

I know, I get it; you're busy! You have errands to run, work to do, appointments to keep, people to see. There are barely enough hours in the day as it is, and now I am asking you to take more time for your life. But here is the reality check; how much time do you spend daily deciding what to wear in the morning? What about deciding what to have for lunch or dinner? What movie you're going to see? Or what about planning your last vacation? And how much time do you spend reviewing your dreams, your goals and your desires and actively planning your life?

Most of us put more time and energy into doing the laundry, and daily household chores, than we do into creating a life plan that inspires us, and developing action steps to get there. Even working in the self-development field, I sometimes find myself guilty of just this. Whenever I feel lost, overwhelmed, or like I'm spinning my wheels, I know it's because I'm not taking enough time for my life.

Generally, we can live our lives by design or by default. We can make a plan, set targets and work towards them, or pray to be happy and hope that things work out. I'm sure you can guess which is likely to produce the best results. Undoubtedly, default *can* be fun in the moment! It can feel spontaneous and full of adventure!

And I highly recommend having an element of this in your life. But most of the time, default just means on auto-pilot; getting through one day at a time without a clear vision for the future. As a day to day lifestyle, it can leave you feeling like you are wandering, at the whim of every passing storm, and somewhat purposeless. In the long run it can produce more anxiety than the alternative. So are you prepared to take a little time for your life?

Coaching Exercise 1:
Start with a plan. Set aside about 30 minutes to do this - and if you're already panicking and thinking that you don't have 30 minutes, a few alarm bells should be going off :)
I like to create a plan at the beginning of every year and again every month. Don't sweat it, I've got you covered! To help you with this I've created **2 easy to fill in templates** for both. Obviously the year long plan is a more involved and will take more time. Both of these are available as FREE DOWNLOADS from my website. See the **Book Bonus Page** at the back of this book to get all the details.

Make it real. Now that you've taken time to create a plan, the magic lies in the implementation. Start by taking small action steps, personally and professionally, and I recommend taking on only one or two major areas at a time. If you are looking for another fabulous coaching tool to help you with this I highly recommend my *New Daily Habit Tracker*. It's also available as a free download with the *Yearly & Monthly Planning Sheets.*

Enjoy the time you take. This is it! The big go-around. Even if you believe in reincarnation, this seems to be the only lifetime you'll remember; the one you're living. It's easy to get caught up, in the daily whir of everyday life, and yes careers and goals. Take some time. Time for you to enjoy the life you have created and are creating. At the end of your life, do you really want to look back at all the time you spent reading emails? What would be the moments that you would cherish the most, and are you doing everything you can now to create them?

Coaching Exercise 2:

Take 5-10 minutes and answer the following questions. List 3 things for each area.

1. What is really working for you in your life right now?

2. Is there anything you need to do to maintain or add to this?

3. What are you unhappy with and what isn't working?

4. What are the steps you can take to clean this up or eliminate it?

5. What would you love to be doing that you're not? And how can you move closer to that by the end of the month?

Affirmation:

"I choose to make my life a priority."

P.S. I've written more on affirmations in section 25 of this book. There are also some printable Affirmation Cards available in the Book Bonuses section as well

Part II
Easier, Better, Faster

8. Life Is Not an Emergency

"Unease, anxiety, tension, stress, worry... all forms of fear... are caused by too much future, and not enough presence."
- Eckhart Tolle

At one point today, I was seriously overwhelmed. I had lunch with a girlfriend and indulged in 2 cups of coffee - not the norm for me. Soon I found my pulse racing, I couldn't concentrate and panic set in. My mind was going 90 miles an hour, scanning everything I had to do, and I could feel my breath quicken. I stopped, tried to breathe slowly, and attempted to figure out what this was all about.

I wanted to rush back to the office and my computer and dive into the day's work. Instead, I kept repeating, "Life is not an emergency." If that was true, why was I feeling such sudden irrepressible anxiety?

When I did get back to my desk, I decided to read an article from a favorite spiritual teacher who writes and speaks about love's power to heal, and is generally very soothing. Today she talked about *"urgency, the worldwide crisis and call to action, meeting global timelines, pressuring our leaders, not moving fast enough, and an immediate appeal"*. Hmmmm... Then I went to my inbox, (in the ever persistent flood of emails) this is what I found: *"Register Today. For a Limited Time Only. Sale ends tomorrow at noon. Last chance to buy before it's taken off the market for good. Act now. This is a one time offer"*. Seeing a pattern?

Even at the gym; which is the stop I opted for before returning from lunch, thinking that the workout would calm my frazzled nerves; over the PA they continually announced a *"one day sale"* on their latest package, and the girls behind the desk made sure to let me know, on my way in, and my way out, that there were extra benefits if I signed up now.

Since when did life become such an emergency? Why are we expected to do, be, have, accomplish and *buy* everything right now? And I mean today. This moment.

Any parent will tell you that the childhood years go by too fast, and they cherish so many of those fleeting moments. And do we really want to rush a kiss? A favorite movie? Fireworks? Or any of life's other delectable events? Why is it then that we try to go through it at break-neck speed doing everything yesterday? The finish line in this one is kind of final, so what are we really rushing towards? Or are we just rushing?

We are so afraid of not keeping up, not staying on top, not getting it all done. But in our fear and panic, what do we miss along the way? Life is like a sumptuous meal, shared with good friends, even the odd bitter bites are not as unpleasant when taken with a sense of ease. And the delicious ones, all the more savory. This is not an emergency.

Today, this week, this month, or whenever you feel like it, I hope you can allow yourself a few extra moments of peace. Allow yourself to unhook from the "emergencies" of life. Allow yourself to "not get there" today, and to just be, and know that's enough. The ride doesn't stop even when we take a break, and a few moments breather may give you the extra strength you need to hold on for another whirl around.

We are continually pressured to move faster and faster, being reminded of missed opportunities and last chances. But isn't it exhausting? And really, you can't do it all anyway; and who wants to? In case no one else has given you permission, be selective, slow down… It's okay to take time to breath.

There are no challenges, or assignments, or homework this time, just deep peace and love. After all, isn't that what we're in this for anyway?

9. Staying Focused

"If you don't run your own life, someone else will."
*- **John Atkinson***

It seems that lately you can't turn on the TV or the radio, or even much talk to anyone without hearing about the recession, financial hardships or general economic disaster. We all seem to know someone, who knows someone who has been devastated by the recent turn of events in our financial markets.

But historically, every downturn has eventually been followed by an upturn. This certainly holds true in financial markets, and in my experience, also in our personal lives. The key is to weather life's storms gracefully, keeping a positive and realistic perspective. Being able to do so will not only leave you feeling happier and healthier, but it will also allow you to maintain greater control over the outcome of unsettling events in your life. Here are a few tips to help you stay focused through life's turbulence and storms, whatever they may be.

Keep your emotions in check. While I understand the desire to yell, scream, rant, rave, cry or otherwise vent, this is going to do very little to solve the immediate problem. As a matter of fact, an emotional response immediately puts your body into fight or flight mode, reducing your reasoning abilities, and impairing your judgment. This is no way to handle a problem. While I wildly encourage you to "let it all out", as strange as this may sound, set a time limit on it. Cry, whine, blow off steam, but then let it go and come back to the matter at hand with a cooler head and a bit more determination. Strong emotional reactions are nature's way of letting us know that something is terribly wrong, but an emotional response is not a great tool for governing our lives.

Just the facts. The best way to get yourself out of an emotional response is to take a very clear look at the facts. Get out a pen and paper, and write down what is going on. If it's financial difficulties you are experiencing, take the time to do a current statement of net worth, evaluate your spending and your saving patterns. Having this information plainly in front of you will allow you to make clearer and sounder judgments on what the next best step is.
I know this can be challenging if you're wound up, so take it in bite sized pieces, maybe 30 minutes at a time if you need a mental health break.

Keep your eye on the prize. Remember those goals you set earlier in the year? Whenever you're facing a challenge in any area of your life, go back to your goals – what is it that you really and truly want? What are you willing to work for?
If you're having relationship difficulties, ask yourself if your current relationship is truly reflecting where you see yourself in the long term? If it is, how can you work through the current situation, and if not, is it time to gently let it go?

No snap decisions or sudden moves. It's really easy when we get into "crisis mode" to make a snap decision. Your boss ticks you off yet again today, and you decide that this is the last time! But ask yourself if that snappy comeback is worth the backlash, or if quitting is really going to make it any easier to pay your mortgage or your rent. Take some time; assess the situation, and then act. You'll be clearer and calmer the next day, and if you don't feel as impassioned then, maybe it wasn't such a big deal after all, or there is another way to handle it.

Show a little discipline. When we're stressed out, on edge, and ready to snap, focusing on our goals, putting it in writing and counting to ten may be the very last thing we want to do, but trust me, it's worth it. Now more than ever it's important to stick to your guns. Being able to exercise a little discipline may be all it takes to keep a bad situation from becoming a disaster, and in the end it separates the men from the boys, and the women from the girls.

Seek new information and get some support. I believe it was Einstein who once said that it is your current level of thinking that got you to exactly where you are right now. Sometimes it's okay to rely on someone else's thinking to take you a little bit further. Whatever your challenge or situation, getting a little more info can only help. Read up, become better educated and better informed. Seek out a mentor, an advisor, or hire a coach.

Coaching Exercise: Take any current situation that is stressing you out, or driving you crazy right now, and follow the steps above. Allow yourself some time for new answers, new awareness and greater clarity to appear. Being able to move forward in the face of adversity can leave you with an amazing sense of power and freedom, and new found strength.

10. Detox Your Inbox

"If E-mail had been around before the telephone was invented people would have said "Hey, forget e-mail - with this new telephone invention thing, I can actually talk to people."
*- **unknown***

How many emails are currently in your inbox? And how much anxiety does this produce? More and more one of the biggest stressors that I see with clients is the never ending flood of emails. For most of us, they come in at a rate that we can't possibly manage if we were to try and read and respond to every single one. The inability of which can gnaw away at your sense of accomplishment and control. When time is so precious, one of the biggest culprits and thieves seems always to be email.

Do you remember when you first started using email… roughly? Or more to the point, do you remember a time when you didn't use it? Most of us can answer yes to both of those questions. There was no email or internet when we were kids – at least not in the form that we use it today. So is it any wonder that so many of us are on email overload? We have ridiculously long list of emails in our inboxes, and no matter how much time or energy we spend on answering them it never seems to be enough.

But we didn't come into the world using email. Our parents didn't use it. As a matter of fact, most of us got our folks going on this whole internet thing.

So is it any wonder that we're struggling with multitudes of messages? Here are a few tips to help you "detox your inbox" and spend less time in front of your computer and more time living your life!

Short and Sweet. This is truly a case where less is more! Remember that everyone else is in the same email situation. Most of us get more emails than we can possible get through in one day. This inevitably leads to a backlog. Don't ramble on with long paragraphs. Keep it short and to the point – use bullet lists when you can. You'll more than likely find that people are not offended by your brevity, but thankful for it!

Choose and Change Your Title. How many times have you gone through your deleted or sent items folder looking for a particular email, only to find it with some obscure title about something that had happened a week earlier? When creating your emails, use a descriptive title – we're all thankful for that! And when responding, if you're changing the content, change the title too (this is one of my personal pet peeves!) It takes only seconds, but can save precious minutes later, and when we're all dealing with the volume of email that we are, these minutes easily turn into hours.

Ask for Action. Do you need a response? Is there a deadline? Do you NOT need a response? Including this information in your title line can make things easier and less frustrating for everyone. Here are some examples including the following information after the regular title:
NO RESPONSE REQUIRED
PLEASE SUBMIT BY 5 PM
PLEASE RESPOND

I found these especially useful when emailing groups and communication can go a little awry.

Pick and Choose. As I mentioned earlier, most of us receive more emails than we can possibly read every day. As I stared one morning with an inbox with 97 waiting messages, I did the math on how long it would take me to answer or "deal with" each one. I realized that at 5 minutes per message, (some taking 2 minutes, others 20) it would take me a little more than 8 hours to empty my inbox – assuming that no more came in during that time! We simply can't read and respond to everything. That is when I aggressively adopted the next Rule…

Diligently Delete. What do you need to read today? What do you really want to? What could you let go of and not miss? Ask yourself: Is it fun? Is it useful? Is it necessary? Will it change my life? If not, can you let it go?

How we spend our time is how we spend our lives. Do you want to look back at your life years from now and remember how much time you spent emailing? So clear it up, cut it down and aim for Zero Inbox!

11. Planning Your Day The Night Before

"Meticulous planning will enable everything a man does to appear spontaneous."
- **Mark Caine**

One of the best pieces of advice that a coach ever gave me was "Never begin your day before it's finished on paper." Over the years, this has served me extremely well. Whenever my day is not flowing smoothly, or I'm generally unproductive or "feeling a little lost" chances are it is due to poor preparation. This is equally common with the hundreds of clients I've worked with. But I've also discovered that preparing for stellar days goes way beyond the to-do list. There are also mental and physical components. A few small, minor modifications can yield outstanding results. Here are some of my favs.

The List. I know, I know. I've said before that the to-do list wasn't the be-all-to-end-all, but it *is* important. Again, "Don't begin your day until it's finished on paper." Take 5 or 10 minutes the night before and write down what you need to do the next day. Make sure that the 3 to 5 most important or "must do" items are at the top of the list. Draw a horizontal line dividing the page, and everything else that would be *nice* to get done falls below that line.

When you get up in the morning concentrate on the most important items first! It is also really important to do this list the night before. This gives your brain the chance to mentally prepare for the day ahead. You're also far less likely to lie awake in bed at night going over what you have to do the next day – it's already done!

Prep the Morning Ritual. Do you routinely skip breakfast because there's not enough time? Are you rushing to get the kids ready? Or make lunch? Do this kind of prep the night before. If you drink coffee in the morning, (and I whole heartedly suggest that you switch to non-caffeinated herbal tea :), make sure that the coffee maker is set-up and ready to go at the touch of a button. Lay out place mats, dishes and cutlery for breakfast, and do whatever food prep you can. You can even put cereal in the bowls (covered of course!) This is a wonderful way to begin the day feeling nourished, cared for and ready to take on the world.

Where's the Wardrobe? How many times have you been getting dressed in the morning only to discover that the shirt you were going to wear is at the dry cleaners? You can't find the necklace that perfectly accessorizes your outfit? Or, ladies – no pantyhose to be found anywhere!
Spend a few minutes the night before and gather your clothes for the morning. Actually take them out of the closet, make sure everything is there, clean, functional and in "good working order." This can save you a lot of stress and last minute panic if something just doesn't go right!

Set Two Alarms. Yup! You read it right! This little trick has afforded me many a good night's sleep. Especially when traveling. Have you ever "slept through the alarm", just not set the clock right, or had a mid night power outage wreak havoc with the clock radio? What about waking up every 30 minutes paranoid that you're going to miss your flight or sleep through a big meeting? If you need an alarm to get up in the morning, (many don't, but many do), why not set two?

Set them about 10 minutes apart so you're not startled with them both going off at the same time. Use one that is tied into the electrical power, and another, such as a cell phone or good old fashioned alarm clock that is not. The chances of both alarms failing are pretty slim and you can get a good night's sleep knowing that you'll be up on time – no matter what!

Relaaaaaax! Do you read murder mysteries in bed at night? Watch TV? Surf the internet? Your brain needs time to wind down, and to produce enough serotonin to ensure that you sleep soundly through the night. This is only possible if you stop the input of stimulus and reduce the amount of light being processed through the retina. So allow yourself at least 30 minutes to wind down. Turn off the tube, slip out of cyberspace and put down the books.

This is a great time to do the prep that I mentioned above. Done repeatedly, this will act as a signal to your brain that we're coming up on time to sleep and allow it to make the necessary shifts – mentally and chemically for this part of your day.

Put Stuff Away. Last but not least, take a few minutes and do a quick tidy up! Put away any small items lying around, load up the dishwasher, straighten your desk (if you work from home) and create a sense of order and peace. It's wonderful to go to bed knowing that this is done, and absolutely lovely to wake up to!

Whenever I don't do these things, I find that my productivity the next day falls by about a whopping 70%. And yes, you guessed it, the stress level goes up about the same. A nighttime ritual is really a gift that you give yourself. It's not only efficient, but it creates an incredible sense of calm and order and peace in an otherwise hectic world.

12. New vs. Necessary

*"When faced with a challenge, look for a way,
not a way out."*
- **David L. Weatherford**

Just for today, assume that I have nothing new to tell you.
Assume that you've read it, seen it and heard it all before. In
an era of information overload, this is an easy assumption to
make.
Every year hundreds of new self-help books, diets, and
financial fads hit the market. Yet every year, more and more
people struggle with depression, excess weight, and mounting
debt. So where is the problem and what is the solution? Do
the books lie? Are they filled with bad advice and untruths?
With so much great guidance out there, where are we all
going wrong? It's simple; we're looking for something new.
How many times have you faced a problem in life, read
everything you could on the subject, talked to anyone who
would listen, and still found nothing new? It's the same advice
over and over. And how many times have you diligently acted
upon the advice that was given? Most of us figure that if we've
heard it before, we're automatically doing it.

Not so. Advice is no less valuable because it's recurring.
Actually, that's a pretty good sign that it's sound. Good advice
appears again and again because it is ignored – again and
again, even by those who are giving it!
Let's face it, there's enough information out there to resolve
most of our human dramas, yet they perpetuate in the face of

overwhelming tools to solve them. We take comfort in the fact the "we know" what to do, and therefore we must be doing it. But the reality is knowing is only knowing. The actual "doing" can be uncomfortable, unpleasant, or downright difficult, so we look for something new instead of just doing what is necessary.

Most of us know what the necessary steps are to at least begin to solve the problem at hand; losing weight, saving money, or dealing with a difficult relationship to name a few, but often those steps aren't fun, glamorous, easy or sexy. If they were, we would have already done them.
So my challenge to you this week is to pick an area of your life where you feel frustrated or stuck; where you're looking for something new, and ask yourself if you honestly know what it is that you could or should be doing? Ask yourself what is necessary, and just do it! Assume that you haven't been acting on any of the advice that you've been getting, and if you are acting on some of it, but still not getting the results you want, then just do a little more.

New and different have their place, only after we have mastered the old and necessary, in our businesses and in our lives. So for now, have fun! Learn heaps! And do what's Necessary before the New!

13. Urgent vs. Important

"For fast acting relief, try slowing down!"
- Lily Tomlin

How many times have you felt that there just aren't enough hours in the day? How often have you rearranged your schedule and rewritten your to-do list to deal with a pressing situation or "something that just came up"? Although time may seem like the issue, I'm willing to bet it's more about what you choose to make urgent, and what is really important.
Everyday there are deadlines to meet, and "fires to put out". Something and someone is always begging for our attention, time and energy. But the reality is there is only so much to give. We each get 168 hours a week. That's it. No more. How you choose to use your 168 hours will determine the quality of your life, and your long-term overall happiness.

So why is it that some people with their 168 hours can write books, build fortunes and break records, while others can barely survive to collapse in exhaustion at the end of the day? It all lies in what you choose to make "urgent" and what you choose to make "important".
Urgency, in my experience and working with clients, tends to stem from one of two things – somebody else's need or our own fears. Recently I calculated that if I dealt with every "urgent" email that came across my desk every day, it would take me roughly 7½ hours (every day!) to deal with what other people feel is urgent. Yet only a fraction of these emails actually reflected what to me, in my life, is truly important.

The other reason for urgency is fear. We tend to feel that something is urgent when there is a time limitation involved. Advertisers use this all time to get us to make impulse purchases on "limited time offers". When there is a chance we could miss an opportunity, or lose out on something, or even risk someone's disapproval, suddenly the issue becomes urgent.

This week, take a few moments and really evaluate what in your life is important, and based on that, decide what you feel is urgent. Make a list of everything that is important to you in your life right now. It may look something like this:
- Taking care of my health.
- Building my career.
- Spending more time with my family.
- Getting enough sleep.
- Losing weight.
- Saving more money.

Write as many things as you can think of. Now go through your list and put stars beside the top 10 or top 6 - depending how long your list is. Now put an extra star beside the top 3.

Write these three things down on a sticky note and put it on your desk, in your wallet or on your bathroom mirror; somewhere that you can see it every day. This is what you've decided is really important to you right now. When a decision is to be made over whether or not something is urgent, consult your list. Does it move you further towards what is on that list? Is there a negative consequence from not addressing it immediately?
If the answer isn't yes to either one of these questions, then it probably isn't really urgent. As you complete your top three

objectives, move on to the next.

When I first started coaching, I worked with a particular client who was always exhausted, running late, had little time for sleep and still never seemed to be getting ahead. I asked her to do this exercise and differentiate between what was urgent and what was truly important for her. When we looked at her list of what was currently going on, as well as what had occupied her time in the last couple of weeks, we found that in this case, urgent and important were often the same thing. This client had two teenage boys who always seemed to be "getting into situations". Her husband was frequently away on business leaving her to pick up the majority of the parenting responsibilities. For her, her sons were of paramount importance, but also creating a majority of the urgent situations. And to top things off, she was the primary breadwinner in the family, which added to the pressure and stress. Doing this exercise allowed her to gain clarity of the situation and to put some structures in place to deal with it. Knowing that her family's well-being was so important to her, but she also needed to increase her income, she immediately hired more help around the house, gave her sons more responsibility and put stricter consequences in place for any out-of-line behavior. She also had heart-felt talks with her sons bringing them in on the big picture. They came to participate in the family's overall health and happiness as a whole, learning valuable skills for later in life.

Letting go of the urgent and fully embracing the important is what allows us to live richer and more rewarding lives. So take a deep breath, let go of the urgent, and enjoy doing what you find to be truly important. This is not only where the success, but also where the joy lies!

14. Overcoming Procrastination

"Procrastination is the art of keeping up with yesterday."
- Don Marquis

We all do it. We put it off. Push it back. Wait. Hope. Agonize. And in the eleventh hour, at the last moment, or when we just can't stand to live with it any longer, we finally get it done! This is the anatomy of procrastination.

Procrastination is one of the biggest dream killers out there. It diminishes opportunities, thwarts our progress, keeps us stuck in the past and sets us up for failure. I recently came across a great quote from the author William James, "Nothing is so fatiguing as the eternal hanging on of an uncompleted task." Oh so true. How much time do you spend thinking about what you have to do, as opposed to just getting on with it and doing?

Whatever it is, it just sits there in the back of our consciousness nagging and moaning, taking up valuable energy and thought-space. It robs us of fully enjoying the present moment and depletes our inner peace. So with so many negative consequences, why do we all do it, and how do we stop? Why do we continue to punish ourselves with procrastination?

Procrastination has many voices, and they sound something like this; "I'll get to it as soon as I can, or as soon as I've finished this. It can wait a little bit longer. There will still be enough time later or tomorrow. I don't know where to begin. I don't feel like it." Or my personal favorite, "Somehow it'll get done," even when there's no one else to do it!

These are the lies we tell ourselves, and not with the intention of punishment, but to keep ourselves safe. We only don't do something when there is an imagined negative outcome, or somehow a perceived risk. So why wouldn't we want to move forward in our business, deepen our relationships, improve our health or our finances? Simple. What if we fail?
In working with clients, and in my own life, I've found that the underpinnings of procrastination are always fear based. Even when writing this book, I have found myself stalling, worried that when I sit down to type, I'll have nothing to say, (my close friends are giggling out loud right about now!)

So what is it that worries you? Where are you afraid to fail? Is it the fear of rejection in a relationship? Messing up if your business grows too much? Finding a health problem on an annual doctor's visit? Or generally being found out as not good enough? We all have something, and for most of us many things, but avoiding them will never make them go away. It only means that the fears, large and small, get to continue to run your life, and more often than not, run it down.

My challenge to you this week is to pick just one thing, and stop procrastinating. Maybe it's a communication that you need to deliver, paperwork that needs to be done, a dentist visit or eye exam, or cleaning up your finances. Whatever it is, pick one thing, and like Nike says, "Just do it!"

Whatever you dread doing most this week, is probably the thing that is going to move you forward the quickest. It will free up time and mental energy, and pave the way for more good to come in. Confronting issues, people or situations is never fun, but it pales in comparison to the ongoing pain of uncertainty, and the heaviness one feels with issues hanging over their head.

So for now, get it done, lighten up and treat yourself to a little relief by busting your own procrastination.

15. Great Beginnings

*"Success is deciding from the start what end result
you want and creating the circumstances
to realize that result."*
- **Mark Victor Hansen**

How did you begin your day today? What about yesterday?
And the day before? Do you have a set pattern, habit, or
routine? Do you start your day purposefully and deliberately,
or simply jump out of bed with the jolt of the alarm?
Great movies and books have careful and clever beginnings.
They are written and edited to grab our attention, and to set
the stage for what is to come. In essence, they create the tone
and feeling for our experience. So what kind of days do you
create for yourself?
Most people begin their days by default. Yes, I said by default.
Because when we're not consciously creating, that's exactly
what we're doing. We place ourselves at the mercy of the
whims of the day, allowing whatever mood or emotion is
closest to govern our experiences and shape our lives. So if
movies and books deserve carefully planned beginnings,
doesn't your one, and only precious life? We don't get to
choose our initial start in life, but we can choose how we begin
each new day.
Motivational Speaker and Success Guru Tony Robbins, starts
his day by asking himself an empowering question, like: "What
am I most excited about today?"
The Dalai Lama begins each morning at 4am in prayer and
meditation.

And how do you think these processes change and shape their lives? How could a similar process shape yours?

So this week can you begin to consciously create your days? Begin by just observing for a few days what do you do each morning? How does it feel? And how does it shape, or frame your day? If you don't already have a powerful centering, grounding or motivating ritual for the morning, could you start one?

Here are a few of my favorite ways to begin my day:
- With a 5-10 minute meditation for peace, abundance and all good things.
- Writing 2 or 3 pages in a journal to get thoughts, feelings and "stuff" out on paper and clear the mind.
- Reviewing my current "Big Goal" and dreaming up new ways to achieve it.
- List 5 or more things that I'm truly and deeply grateful for.
- Making the bed, lighting incense and clearing the space for new energies to come in.

This week I invite you to take a little more control of your life. Create a process that you can do within moments of awakening, to guide and shape your days. The simpler the better, and sticking with it is important – everyday for at least a week or two. Begin to notice how your new ritual impacts your life and your interactions with those around you. Whatever you do, the main thing is to decide today how you will begin your day tomorrow!

16. Rich People Time Management

"The difference between poor people and rich people is that poor people spend their money and invest what's left over; rich people invest their money and spend what's left over."
Jim Rohn

One of the issues that comes up most often in coaching is time management. People are always looking for new and better ways to get more done! Ironically, everyone I know - friends, family and clients, are all super busy. But there's a difference between just being busy, and being productive. Getting more out of your life isn't just getting more stuff done; it's getting the right stuff done. And in my opinion, it's also enjoying life as you do it. So what exactly is the right stuff?

How do we begin to prioritize our days and the tasks at hand when so many things seem to be screaming for our attention? The first thing I always encourage is a long range plan. You can't possibly make effective and satisfying decisions about how or where to spend anything - time, money, or energy; unless you know what you're working towards.
You probably wouldn't get in your car and drive 24 miles or kilometers in any given direction with no particular destination in mind, other than to get through the ride, any more than you would hand over $24 just to get it out of your wallet, without expecting to get something back for it.

Yet we routinely give up our precious 24 hour days in this very manner; trying to 'get through' them instead of live them, enjoy them, and use them up fully!

Once you know where you're going, it's time to break this into bite-sized pieces and take a hard look at priorities. If you've made a five year plan, break it down to one year, and then what is your specific goal for this month? From here we can decide on our actions steps and then get going.

Instead of the usual long 'To Do' list of everything you'd like to/need to get done, begin by making a list of everything that is needed to bring you closer to the current month's goals. Be brutally honest, what is important? Is it important to sign new clients? Get the house in order? Spend more time relaxing and with the kids? Maybe get a new job or a higher earning position? Pick one or two major things per month - that's plenty! Any more and you're setting yourself up for failure, disappointment, and of course, not enough time.

Once you have the major goals and the actions you intend to take, you can then allocate several to each week. That's enough. There will be plenty of other things that come along to fill in your days. Getting these big things done places a higher value on your time, and they're what are really going to move you forward personally and professionally. The added little bonus that I often see with this is an increase in self-esteem. When we do what we say we're going to do, we trust ourselves more and value our time more. The more we trust ourselves and value our time, the more we can do, which increases our confidence and self-esteem, and so it goes.

Time is the great equalizer; we all get 168 hours in a week - no more, no less. It doesn't matter if you're an internet billionaire or a struggling waitress or bartender; we all get the same number of hours in a day. So what we do with that time really counts. And does just knowing that make you value your own time just a little bit more?

We can't get everything done, and who wants to? So why not decide what's important, what lights you up, and what's going to move you in the direction of your dreams, and let whatever else you can, go?

The quote from Jim Rohn at the beginning about money, also applies to time. Rich people invest first in what's important to them, and then spend the rest. So what do YOU really want to do with YOUR time? It is our one finite resource - the thing that we can not buy more of, manufacture or even save up for a rainy day, so how do you want to spend yours?

17. Shiny Object Syndrome

"Some people plant in the spring and leave in the summer. If you've signed up for a season, see it through. You don't have to stay forever, but at least stay until you see it through."
*- **Jim Rohn***

Are you one of those people who just wants to do EVERYTHING? Love to start projects, but have a tough time completing? And if so, my guess is that you're prone to feeling stressed out, overwhelmed and run down. Take heart, you're in good company! Yours truly over here suffers the same; yes, a true case of Shiny Object Syndrome.

Most of you probably know the signs; you hear something, you see something, you get a new and brilliant idea that you can't wait to get started on! You drop everything and off you go on the latest and greatest and newest idea. Fast forward a few weeks, or maybe months, and the "shiny new idea" isn't so shiny or new anymore. As a matter of fact it has lost a lot of its luster, and looks, feels and smells a lot like hard work. It's not as interesting as you thought it would be, and definitely not as much fun! This isn't what you signed up for! Sound familiar?

Shiny Object Syndrome is not uncommon; as a matter of fact it seems to be running rampant in this instant gratification, newer is better, ADD society. It's marked by moments of excitement and inspiration, followed by the plunge into boredom and the mundane.

So how do we combat this roller coaster cycle, and actually follow through, complete what's most important to us, and get stuff done? Here are a few tips that I've used in my own ADD-ish life and with "highly curious" clients ;)

Stick to a Schedule. If you suffer from Shiny Object Syndrome, a vague and long "To Do" list isn't going to cut it; you'll simply pick something from the list at random because "you feel like it" and before you know it you're wandering throughout your day. This leisurely approach feeds your distraction while tricking your brain into believing that you're being productive. Write down what you're going to do and WHEN and then stick to it!

Check Email at Set Times. This is the most pervasive and un-shiny of the shiny objects. It's constant, always new, demands immediate attention (woo hoo! exciting!), but really in the end is very un-shiny. Emails are generally other people's wants, needs, demands and problems. Us SOS people check it hoping for something interesting and usually just end up with more work and things to deal with. This can leave you feeling distracted, bored and overwhelmed. Solution: Set specific times during the day to deal with emails. Allocate 15-20 minute time slots and stick to it. You'll be amazed at how much you can get done in so little time.

Stop Responding to Other Shiny Objects. I keep a sticky note on my computer - just one, only one. And all it says is "I do complete work." That is a mantra one of my first coaches gave to me, and yes, I need CONSTANT reminding!
When you have the urge to mentally wander off onto another projected or great idea, stop, breathe, and repeat that out loud. Breathe again, and resume the task at hand. It'll go far quicker than picking it up later after dropping it halfway through.

Get Help. I know this sounds funny, but it's really true... but maybe not in the way you're thinking! When you get another brilliant idea or have found a new shiny object, run it by a colleague, a coworker, a business partner, family member or friend. Get them to take 5 minutes to walk you through the steps to completion. I bet you it's not that shiny anymore. If it still is, then schedule it in around other priorities and THEN act on it.

Shiny Object People are the dreamers, the motivators the energizers in our society! Some people are great with ideas. Other people are better with the follow through. Whichever you are, love it, enjoy it and cherish it! We need all of us in this world to keep it beautiful and unique and in constant motion. If you're a Shiny Object Person, surround yourself with people who aren't; they'll ground you and stabilize your brilliant ideas. And if you're a No-Distraction-Get-it-Done Type, (please, I need to hire you!) have a bit of patience with your Shiny Object friends; they'll keep you amused, entertained and inspired!!

18. Taking Action

*"When we put action behind our positive thinking, it
will spur change in our life that seems like magic."*
- ***Rhonda Britten***

People come to coaching for all sorts of reasons, but the
common denominator is that there is something that they want
that they're just not getting! It may be more money, a better
relationship, greater success in their career or business or a
deeper sense of peace and well-being.
One thing I see over and over again, are well-meaning men
and women who have "tried everything" but still can't seem to
get exactly what they want. They have read a dozen or more
books, made as many plans, crafted vision boards, chanted
mantras, done affirmations, begged, pleaded, bargained with
and prayed to the 'powers that be' and still all of these efforts
have turned up virtually nothing. Exhausted and frustrated,
they ask "What am I doing wrong? Why isn't this working?"
The answer: it's all about taking action.

I think it was Jim Rohn who said *"The world doesn't pay you
for what you know, it pays you for what you get done."* Even if
you're a teacher or an author, you only get paid when you
actively share that knowledge; you've got to prepare and give
that lecture, or write the book - in other words take action.

So often we kid ourselves; we think that knowing and planning
is enough. It's not. We read book after book on relationships,
money, time management or even meditation, but fail to put
the knowledge into measurable actions. You may know how to

make a sandwich, but if you're hungry, the knowing alone is not going to get you fed! Planning to make the sandwich, journaling on it or examining your limiting beliefs about hunger isn't going to do the trick.

So to see how well you are with taking action, here's a quick coaching exercise below:
1. Write down an important dream or goal for you right now.
2. On a scale of 1-10, how important is it to you?
3. On a scale of 1-10, how many actions did you take last week to achieve it? Actions - not talking about, analyzing, planning, organizing, praying or hoping, (all valid by the way, just not on their own!)
4. List what the actions were that you took last week in order to achieve this goal or live this dream.

Did the numbers in question 2 & 3 match? And how many actions were you able to list?

Make a list of possible actions you could take this week.
You guessed - pick a couple and get into action.
If you're not getting what you want in some area of your life, chances are you're not taking enough action. Equally important is taking *consistent* action and the *right* actions. So for the next two weeks, I challenge you to focus on that goal, and take consistent daily action. Strive for one solid action step per day, and just see how much your life changes. Write each action down, and at the end of two weeks you'll have the beginnings of a roadmap to success!
If you're not sure of what actions to take, you may need to do more research, enlist the help of a buddy, or of course hire a coach. And you can always post your questions on my Facebook fan page, and I'll be sure to respond.

19. Taming Your To-Do List

"The simple truth is, if you are going to expand your life beyond its current confines, you are going to encounter resistance. The question is, what will you do with it when it shows up?"
- ***The Coach***

So, how long is your "To Do List"? Do you complete it every day? Or does it drag on forever, always increasing, and just never getting done? Too long and never ending "to do" lists are one of those little things that can eat away at your energy, your self-esteem and generally just make life a little less fun. We set ourselves up for failure daily; with things we can't complete and then beat ourselves up later for. But we can break the cycle and move through our list quickly and more effectively by adopting a few small changes in the way we view the tasks at hand.

Write it down. If you haven't already, get it out of your head and on to paper. This will give you a clearer picture of all of your tasks, and allow you to manage them more easily.

Schedule them in. This is key! It may take a few minutes, but I assure you that it's well worth the effort. Take an honest look at each item, and decide how much time it will take, and when would be the best time to do it, whether it's today, this week or this month. For most of us this is a great big reality check when we realize that if you include eating sleeping and other basics, you probably have at least 27 hours worth of goodies on the list for today.

63

When a task is scheduled, it lessens the nagging feeling of it hanging over your head. You know what you need to do, and that it will get done at the allocated time.

Stick to the plan. Once you have things into your schedule, then stick to it. Notice when you try to wriggle out of something or put it off, or even do something else first. It's this kind of avoidance that keeps us stuck and overwhelmed.

Why are you doing this? We can immediately give our actions more power, and find more motivation, if we take a moment to remember *why* this item is on the list to begin with – both short term and long term. This one simple step alone can turn a list of tedious tasks into a compelling agenda.

Here are some examples:
Task: Pay all the bills and file the paperwork
Short Term Benefits: I get to keep the car, the lights stay on, the papers are all off my desk, and best of all, I don't have to think about it for another month
Long Term Benefits: I'll be more organized and less stressed at year end and tax time.

Task: Write the proposal letter/look for a new job
Short Term Benefit: Increased income, better utilize my skills
Long Term Benefit: Achieve my financial goals sooner. Will be able to take an extra trip this year. Retire sooner.

Task: Go to the gym regularly
Short Term Benefit: I'll feel healthier, maybe drop a few pounds, have more energy and look better too!
Long Term Benefit: Helps to prevent degenerative illnesses, has an overall "anti-aging" effect, and will keep me younger,

more flexible and mobile well into older years.

Last year, I was teaching this exercise at a group workshop. A few months later one of the participants emailed me with an amazing success story. With her permission, I've paraphrased the email here:

"Hi Hunter,
Thanks so much for the "Taming Your To-do List" exercise. I finally got around to something on my list that I have been putting off for months...creating my Linked-In profile. I really didn't expect anything to come from it, but I thought there was a longer term benefit. It proved to be much quicker than that! To my surprise I was contacted by a corporate recruiter within a week and offered a job at a competing company. The new position would have been a definite promotion, with a substantial increase in pay and better benefits. I was really hesitant, because I love the company culture where I'm currently employed, but the offer was simply too good to pass up. As a courtesy, I decided to speak with my manager and let her know face to face that I would be putting in my resignation and why. Much to my surprise, my current employer not only matched, but beat the offer! I now have the job of my dreams and I didn't have to move anywhere. This has changed my life, and I can't thank you enough!"

I can't promise that everyone will get a raise and a promotion, from doing this, but we're never really sure of what the long term benefits will be of taking action now. So this week take on your "To Do's". Be brutally honest; schedule in what's most likely to bring you the biggest results and the greatest joy. Give these items priority and notice what changes in your energy and in your life.

Part III
Tending To The
Inner World

20. Reignite Your Passion

"Don't ask yourself what the world needs; ask yourself what makes you come alive. And then go and do that. Because what the world needs are people who have come alive."
- Harold Whitman

What is it that you're passionate about? Do you even remember? Are you living it and breathing it on a day to day basis? Or has it somehow ebbed away?

For most us, our passions get slowly eroded, and the fires fizzle out as life rains on our parade and extinguishes these precious flames. Our passions get buried under a long list of "To-Do's", obligations and other "shoulds" that we take on in seemingly endless amounts. I understand making a living, but what are you striving for if it isn't passion? Why bother with all of the "To-Do's" if the end result isn't joy?

Everyone has their share of the day to day chores and tasks that are less than joyful in and of themselves, but hopefully we're working towards a higher purpose and greater good.

I've been in that place where I've lost the connection with my passion; the days run together, boredom sets in, and suddenly getting out a bed seems to be a monumental chore. But life certainly does not have to continue this way. Passion isn't something that is extinguished all at once. It's more like a fire that dies when no one tends to and feeds the flame.

So what can you do to reconnect with your passion? And how might your life change if you did?

Complete the statements below, and notice what comes up for you. Allow your mind to wander as you fill them out, and remember, there are no right or wrong answers:

When my life was ideal …
If my life was ideal, I'd have, be and do...
I'd really love to…
Someday I will…

Karen, a 41 year old successful executive in the financial industry, took two weeks before she could even begin to give me answers to the statements above. She said it was a huge wake-up call to realize just how far life had gotten off course. Although she had substantial career success, which had allowed her to provide a very good lifestyle for her family, she realized that passion was in short supply. Karen began to make some small, but immediate changes, and planned others for the months ahead. She took time for trips and family excursions that would have been an absolute "no" a year earlier. Her blood pressure has dropped down to a normal range and she's enjoying life more, realizing that work is a means to an end - not the end in itself.

Notice what you wrote in response to the statements above. Did your answers to flow easily? Did they come from your head or your heart? Is there anything there that you've abandoned or given up on that you deeply miss and crave? Are there one or two items that you could choose to move forward with? One idea? A single small step that you could take this week or this month to reclaim your passion? Write the answers down somewhere visible on cool or interesting paper, in ink that you like.
Passion is life blood! It's the spark that drives you forward and the fuel for your soul! Give yourself the gift of reconnecting with your passion. Unearth old dreams, dare to dream new ones and ultimately create a more impassioned future.

21. Finding Your Voice

"The more faithfully you listen to the voice within you, the better you will hear what is sounding outside."
-Dag Hammarskjold

As many of you may, or may not know, my background, in addition to coaching, is that of a classically trained actress. I've worked in film and television, both in front of and behind the camera; and have also done extensive work in voiceovers. Vocal training was one of the most transformative experiences of my life. To speak clearly and with resonance, I had to get clear on the inside, to face up to things that were emotionally terrifying, embarrassing or just plain uncomfortable.
Oddly, life coaching and acting work wonderfully together. To do either one well you must have a love and a fascination for and with people and human behavior. You've got to be willing to dig deep into your own soul, to face your vulnerabilities, to fully express your joy, and to dance with your shadow.
I know that most of you are not going to run out and become actors tomorrow, but "how you do anything is how you do everything." If you are blocked in one area, it goes much deeper than that.

Recently, a former student of mine contacted me with regards to overcoming "blocks" with his voice. I've paraphrased what I said to him, so that I may share it with you. I hope this allows you to find a little more courage and freedom and joy through your own voice and in your own life. Here, with a few modifications, is what I wrote:

"Hi Eric, Yes, I remember your voice very well, and yes there are some blocks in your reads - I get it… I remember being there. I remember being choked up and not being able to make the 'right' sounds come out.

All of our blocks are emotional - they are what we have been stuffing down and holding back for years. We get blocked when we don't know how to let a little bit out without letting EVERYTHING out. You got close when we were working together; I could tell because you skipped a couple of sessions - I often see that when we start to hit too close to home. But, that obviously wasn't the right time. It has got to be in the right environment with the right supports in place. My guess is, now may be it. I don't know what's shifted in your life, but I have the feeling something has changed - or may be about to :)

Are you're ready to have a breakthrough? Are you ready to dive into deep waters? Are you ready to access 'whatever' is in there, not just what you can control? Answer those questions for yourself, not for me, and yes or no is fine. Depending on what the answer is, you'll know what the next best step is.

People often get blocked in wanting to do things "right" or to not look foolish doing it, but it's those actors (those people!) who let go, who live out loud in front of us that we find sexy, irresistible and endearing.

Ask yourself what's important to you? What are you willing to let go of now? And once you can answer those questions honestly, your subconscious will point you towards the best support/help/teacher for you at this time. This can be a really fun and freeing and terrifying process - not unlike a roller-coaster. But as much as we scream, we still love the ride!"

Coaching Exercise: So as your coach, I invite you to look at the blocks in your own life. They may or may not be with your voice, but there are always some there.

What are you stuck on?

When do you get choked up?

What do you need to say and to who?

What's stopping you?

What would you love to scream at the top of your lungs?

Could you do this in your car?

Where would you love to let loose? Have more fun, freedom and joy?

Who or what would help you along the way?

Go through the questions above and take a few minutes to answer them for yourself. Even if you're not an actor and never intend to be, breath work and improv can be great tools to help you connect to the person that is authentically you, and give him or her a space on center stage in your own life.

Feel free to contact me, (contact info at the back of the book), if you have any questions or revelations around this. And in the meantime, jump on the roller coaster, and enjoy the ride! The drops are a little terrifying, but you're always safe, and it makes the wind in your hair at the top especially delicious!

22. Powerful Questions

"The most important words we'll ever utter are those words we say to ourselves, about ourselves, when we're by ourselves."
- Al Walker, Motivational humorist and trainer

People talk to themselves. We all do it every waking minute, of every hour, of every day. If you have any doubts about this, imagine for just a moment that I was to put your mind on loudspeaker? What would it say? Would it be quiet? What would you hear? And what would those around you hear? Our minds are like super-computers; always spinning and whirring, looking for solutions to problems and answers to questions. And for the most part, they're pretty efficient. We input a question, and sooner or later an answer will pop out. The first time around, it may not always be the right answer, or the best one, so we re-input the question until we somehow find better information. But this wonderful efficiency can sometimes backfire.

Have you ever heard yourself utter one of the following questions? *"How could I be so stupid?"* *"Why does this always happen to me?"* Or *"Why can't I get this right?"* Just as with any other question you may pose to your brilliant brain, it is now busy scanning for answers. And guess what – it will find them.

Asking yourself a question is one of the most powerful things you can do. This is like entering something into your own personal search engine. If you even whisper *"How could I be so stupid?"* your brain will busy itself with finding examples to show you just that. The lesson here is to be careful with your questions – especially the ones you ask of yourself. And if you're going to go searching for answers, they might as well be good ones.

My challenge to you is to ask yourself better questions. Pick an area of your life where you feel challenged or stuck, ask yourself powerful, positive questions, listen for the answers and take immediate action to create new results.

To get you started here are some examples.

What is one step could I take in the next 24 hours to…
- reduce exhaustion and overwhelm?
- heal my relationship?
- grow my business?
- get out of debt?
- lose weight and live healthier?
- relieve mounting stress?
- connect with friends?

How can I…
- get more rest and relaxation?
- live a life that's extraordinary?
- create financial prosperity?
- nourish my heart and soul?
- nurture the relationship of my dreams?
- live up to my own potential and brilliance?
- boost my self-confidence or self-esteem?

Positive questions produce positive answers, combined with positive action yields positive results. So pay attention, listen carefully, act wisely and savor the results.

23. The Starving Self

"The first step towards change is acceptance. Once you accept yourself, you open the door to change. That's all you have to do. Change is not something you do. It's something you allow."
-**Will Garcia**

What is it that you just don't have enough of? Is it time? Money? Happiness? Success? Love? Fulfillment? Joy? Security? Sex? Space?

Most of us want more of something. As a matter of fact, most of us want a lot more of a lot of things. We live in a society where more is always better, and better usually means more. Yet no matter how much we get, we continually seem to be starving. We're starved for love, for affection, for wealth and for time. And as we try to soothe this gobbling savage beast inside, we stuff ourselves with whatever is available; food, shopping, sex, petty dramas and the list goes on. We literally bloat ourselves and our lives, with empty calories and empty content, while trying to feed something much deeper within.

So where are you starving? What are you gobbling up on a daily or weekly basis that is leaving you overweight, in debt, buried in clutter, stressed out, time deprived and still depleted and unsatisfied?

Starvation is no longer a disease of Third World and developing countries. It has reached the proportions of Global Epidemic. Although our North American life styles may seem far removed from starvation, I would suggest just the opposite. Our voracious appetites devour anything in their path; food, clothing, cars, media and the list goes on, with little concern for quantity or quality. This type of indiscriminate ravenous consumption is the hallmark of a starving man. So what are we starving for?

To uncover your own "Starving Self", first make a list of all the things that you consume in excess on a weekly basis. Is it binge eating? Is your spending out of control? Maybe it's alcohol, drugs, movies, internet, electronic games – we all have something.
What do you consume in hopes that you'll feel better, but seldom do? What do you gobble up or spend your time, energy and money on, only to find short term gratification, and never the long term fulfillment that we all crave?

Once you have your list, write beside each item how that particular person, thing or activity makes you feel. Here are a few from my list: I feel relieved, beautiful, rewarded, worthy, more alive, cared-for, secure, desired, in-control. Notice that however it's making you feel in the moment, is probably the opposite of what the long term effects are.
For example, impulse buying may make you feel rich and in control in the moment, but when your credit card statement comes in you'll most likely feel depleted and out of control. Next, pick one "feeling" from your list. If it's cared-for, what could you do this week to truly nurture and care for yourself? If it's financially in-control, what one step could you take this week to taking charge of your finances?

When we truly feed our hungry selves, the need to indulge subsides. We nourish that starving place within us, and our cravings dwindle, as we fuel the desires of our hearts and our souls.

24. Values

*"You are where you are because you want to be
there. If you want to be somewhere else,
you'll need to change."*
*- **Mark Victor Hansen***

Much is said and written about values, and most of us feel that ours are strong, moral and just. But it goes deeper than that. What we truly value, is what runs our lives. Whether it's our job, career, family, finances, health, relationships or home life, taking a look at any of these areas will quickly reveal a person's values – even when the area is unhealthy, unhappy or just plain sucks.

But our values come in two levels; what we value for our immediate comfort, and our true values; what we would have if it were easier, more convenient and life was perfect.

Let's take a look at Comfort Values first. If there is any area of your life where you are unsatisfied and just want more, chances are this area is being run by your Comfort Values. These are the ones that keep you lounging on the couch instead of exercising. They keep you glued to a video game instead of reading that book, taking a course or trying something new. Comfort Values encourage us to over-eat, over-spend, stay in bad relationships instead of going it alone, and playing small instead of taking on the extra responsibility and risks required to achieve great things in our lives.

Comfort Values feel warm and fuzzy, and enjoyable in the moment, but placing momentary comfort before your true values only leads to frustration and disappointment down the road.

Our True Values, in opposition to our Comfort Values, don't always feel good or safe. Valuing higher learning, gives us the drive to study instead of spending a night at the pub. Valuing a wealthy future favors saving money over impulse buying. Valuing our health has us choose whole foods over processed meals and sugary snacks. And valuing impossible achievements has us stick our necks out when we're not sure it's safe. So what are your values? Which set are you allowing to dictate your actions and run your life?

To get clear on your values, pick an area of your life where you are experiencing challenges or feeling unfulfilled. Write down what you would love to have this area of your life look like – if you couldn't fail, if life was easier and perfect. This will show you your True Values.

Now write down what this area of your life looks like now. What is happening that you don't like? What do you most want to change? Where are you compromising? Ask yourself: Am I listening to myself, or am I allowing others to sway my opinion, and/or make the decision for me? What isn't perfect? This will expose your Comfort Values; where you are playing it small or playing it safe in hopes of a momentary feel good. The problem with Comfort Values is that they are never very comfortable for very long. Ultimately they keep us stuck and unhappy and longing for more.

Lastly, how could you best take action to improve this? What is one thing you can do this week? Ask the tough questions. Take a close look, and get a little uncomfortable. You'll be glad you did.

You can download your own free **Values Test** on the Book Bonuses Web Page (link at the back of this book). It's simple, only take a few minutes to do and can really help you get clear on what truly dives and motivates you.

25. Affirmations

"Four short words sum up what has lifted most successful individuals above the crowd: a little bit more. They did all that was expected of them and a little bit more."
- **A. Lou Vickery – Writer**

Affirmations are one of the most misunderstood subjects in coaching. They are really nothing more than something you repeat over and over again to yourself. Many of us have a loop of negative affirmations running through our head at any given time. They are old beliefs and thought patterns, often left over from childhood, some that maybe once served us, and others that were just wrong information to begin with.

They might sound something like this; "Life isn't suppose to be easy. I'm always late anyway. It's never worked before. Change is hard. Men are... Women are... Money is... No one is on my side. I never catch a break. I always screw up." And the list goes on.

They're clichés and axioms picked up over the years both as sticky and as useful as chewing gum stuck to the bottom of your shoe. They're not positive or life affirming. They do nothing to motivate or inspire you. They only drain away your energy and keep you struggling and stuck.

So how can you use this to feel energized, joyful, inspired and alive! This is where Positive Affirmations come in. Now that you get the idea how affirmations work, and just how powerful, and pervasive they can be, let's take a look at how to use them to your advantage as opposed to your disadvantage.

The idea is to swap out some of your negative self-talk for something positive. Many people think that affirmations are 'lies' we tell to ourselves, trying to trick our subconscious into feeling better - quite the contrary. They can be something you appreciate, a goal you are working towards or a commitment you've made to yourself. There are a few keys to effectively working with affirmations:

State it positively. Make statements such as 'I'm enjoying a healthier body and lifestyle.' vs 'I'll feel better when I'm not as fat.'

Repeat it often. 200-300 times a day is barely enough. You've got to counteract the sound loop you currently have running, and think of how long some of those have been going on?

Say it with at least a little bit of enthusiasm! Remember when you were a kid and your mom said 'Say it like you mean it!' Yup! Now is the time.
About a week ago a reporter from The Vancouver Province contacted me wanting to get a life coach's perspective on a viral video of a little girl seemingly doing affirmations. To watch the video (and the 2 minutes is well worth it!) visit…
http://youtu.be/qR3rK0kZFkg

And that is how it's done folks! (standing on the bathroom countertop is optional.) If you can't muster up Little Jessica's enthusiasm, I get it. Sometimes all we can manage is the quiet voice of desperation committed to something better. If that's where you're at today, still try. And pat yourself on the back for doing so.

Affirmations can be powerful tools when used consistently and correctly. To help you with this, I've created a beautiful set of 4 Affirmation Cards with 5 affirmations per card.

Download them through the Book Bonus Web Page, (see the Book Bonuses section at the back of this book) print them out and refer back to them at least once per day. They're completely free, and my gift to you.

26. Who Would You Like To Be?

"A person only begins to become the person he or she wants to be, when they cease to remain content to live with the image of the person they've gotten use to being."
- Hunter Phoenix

As much as I'm a fan of detailed lists and planning, I have often found that the same plans, along with New Year's resolutions and goal lists can fall quickly by the wayside. Enthusiasm wears off, the newness begins to fade and we quickly and easily revert to old habits and patterns.

In my experience, lasting and profound change has little if anything to do with a momentary burst of eagerness and much more to do with a sincere and deep desire. This desire cannot be faked or artificially motivated. It is not born out of peer pressure and does not coincide with the calendar year. It doesn't come from duty or discipline, although both can play a part in seeing it through. And true desire rarely involves words like "should" or "have to" or "need".

This desire comes from that place deep inside each and every one of us; that place where dreams dare to dwell and our greatest hopes and fears reside. It's a place that's scary, awe-inspiring, wondrous and beautiful, because it's from this place that all possibilities, and indeed the very blueprint for our best selves and best life, emerges.

So when was the last time you tapped in to this desire? When was the last time that you really asked yourself - allowed yourself, to question who you really want to be?

Most of us have an idea of how we would like our lives to look, how we would like to look, how we would like other people to see us, how we would like our lives to be. We think of people we know, or maybe even celebrities who seem to have great lives.

These are people who are doing things that we would like to do and living lives that we think we'd like to lead. We may long for this, fantasize about it, pretend and even lie in an attempt to convince ourselves and others that the reality we have is good enough, that somehow things will magically work out, or just as bad, that it's too tough or was never meant to be.

But these lies or fantasies are really clues. They're wake-up calls from our unconscious, attempting to spur us into action through our own discontent. When we're ready to admit that what we have just isn't good enough, this isn't what we really wanted, this isn't who we'd like to be, only then are we able to reconnect with that deep desire that can fuel lasting and profound change.

Again, I ask you, who do you want to be? What traits would you like to embody? What kind of life would you like to lead? I'll often tell my clients that we can either serve as a shining example or a horrible warning, and while this may sound a little extreme, it's through this harsh lens of judgment that we tend to view ourselves and others.

Coaching Homework:

I'd encourage you to re-connect with the person you'd really like to be. Pick someone who embodies traits or qualities that you admire and respect. Take a few minutes and list these traits.

Now look at your list like the wake-up call that it's meant to be. What would you have to do to step closer to this? What would have to change in your life for you to be a shining example and not that horrible warning? Pick one or two small steps that you can take this week to begin to make this happen and write them down.

Call a good friend and tell them about what you're going to do. This will help solidify the actions in your mind, "put it out there" in the real world, as well as keeping you accountable

Having a vision of who it is that you want to be, and holding that vision can act as a roadmap, guiding the steps you take and the choices you make in your life. Have fun with this! And enjoy as you step closer to the greatest expression of you, and remember, that I am always here, taking the journey with you.

P.S. Want a little extra help? I've created a Daily Habits Tracking Sheet (again, see the Book Bonus for this). This is the exact one that I use myself to stay focused and on track. It's one page, it's simple, and if you work it, it works.

27. What Do You Expect?

*"You have to expect things of yourself
before you can do them."*
Michael Jordan

Last night I shocked myself! I love it when that happens. I love it when I find out something new about my thoughts and beliefs that can radically change my life. Let me back up a little…

At the moment, I am in the process of formulating some new plans, as well as goals, dreams and desires for the coming year. There is a new business launch coming so I'm busy writing materials, putting together workshops, planning out schedules, reviewing quotes from professionals, and double checking everything to make sure that nothing has been missed - which of course something always is.

So I review and plan and detail everything some more. One of the things I promised myself I would do is to take care of myself during this period of intense activity. That I would "check-in " with myself daily, pay attention to how my body is feeling and take care of it. I would listen to my inner-thoughts, my internal guidance system, my feelings and my intuition. This single commitment to myself has proven to be far more valuable than I ever could have imagined. I am better rested, happier, more productive, and most importantly I feel loved and cared for and deeply respected.

During my "check-in" last night, I was mentally reviewing all of the work I had put into this current project, and what I was hoping and dreaming for. I thought about good scenarios, great scenarios and then the worst case. Then the quiet voice of intuition asked "But what do you expect?" I quickly grabbed my journal, before my mind had time to distract me, and I began to write "I expect..." and just filled in the blank.

I wrote as much as I could as fast as I could, and some of what came out was shocking. What I expected wasn't all rosy and positive! It wasn't kind, or realistic, or based on anything more than fear. What I was expecting wasn't at all expected! How could this be? I know better. I've done the work. I coach other people through these same situations. But there it was; these ugly thoughts and negative expectations, all reflections of my inner doubts and most critical and small self. All designed by my subconscious to keep me stuck and in a "safe" and familiar place. So now a different type of work begins.

Our unconscious thoughts drive our behaviors. If we believe something is going to be hard and may not produce great results, our brains, in order to protect us, will help us find ways to keep from doing it. If we subconsciously believe that a person in our lives is going to be unpleasant to deal with, in spite of us wishing otherwise, we will instinctively treat them defensively, or may avoid contact with them all together. Aligning our thoughts and our beliefs with our conscious actions is a crucial component to success. Uncovering my own dark and debilitating internal chatter may prove to be one of the best things I could do to ensure success.

So what do you expect? I invite you to take just a minute right now, and write down your two most important goals for this year. Below them, write "I expect..." and complete that sentence in as many ways as you can. Notice if your expectations are supportive to your goals, or detrimental? And if they're not supportive, why not? Are you basing your expectations on past situations? Fear? Or solid reason? Is there anything you need to do to foster a more positive anticipated outcome? Are there actions you need to take? Situations or details that you need to deal with? And could you take just one step this week?

You can't fix what you can't find, so awareness is always the first step. Writing solidifies our thoughts and ideas and makes them real. It also gives our subconscious permission to play in the light of day.
Try this for yourself, and if you feel like sharing, please feel free to contact me through my website, **www.HunterPhoenixCoaching.com**; I'd love to hear about your dreams and goals and what you expect!

28. What Is Important to You?

"We are what we repeatedly do. Excellence, then, is not an act, but a habit."
- Aristotle

With schedules tight and many peoples' minds constantly churning on what's next, I'm going to keep this tip short, sweet and to the point. I'm skipping any long pre-amble and jumping right into a coaching exercise designed to help you gain some clarity and maybe even refocus.

This will require a pen and paper and about 10 minutes of your time. I'd really encourage you not to read ahead, and to do this exercise as it is laid out, to get the maximum benefit from it, (now be honest, if this was one of those redundant circulating emails promising to reveal your personality type as it relates to a series of questions about color choices or animals, wouldn't you take the time and follow the instructions? And yes, this is just as astonishingly accurate!)

First
Take out the pen and make a list of all the things you have to/want to/should do right now. By "right now" I mean anything that is on your radar for the next week. Don't worry about categorizing the list and it certainly doesn't have to be pretty, just write it out; as much as you can think of, as quickly as you can. Give yourself 5 minutes to do this, no more.

Next
Put the to-do list away for a few minutes. Turn it over or put it

under a stack of papers where you can't see it and just put it out of your mind, (that should already leave you feeling a little better!)

Continuing

Now take out a separate sheet of paper and write this heading across the top: What is most important to me right now? Allow yourself another 5 minutes and complete this. Notice what kind of things are making it on your list. Some examples might be: spending more time with my family, eating better, saving more money, finally getting in shape, quitting smoking, taking a vacation, etc.

Side By Side

Once you've complete both lists, I want you to put them side by side on the table. Compare the two. Is your to-do list feeding your 'what's most important' list? Meaning are all, or even some of the items on your to-do list going to help you to create what's most important to you in your life right now? Or is it simply a list of duties, obligations, time-fillers and fluff? Most often we tend to fill our schedules with things that ultimately aren't going to get us to where we want to go. Things that keep us running around, perpetually "busy" and safe from taking that great leap toward what it is that is really going to change our lives.

To Finish

From your 'what's most important' list, pick one thing; the one thing that would improve your life the most if you achieved it, got it done or moved forward on it. Now revise your to-do list to reflect this. Take out some of the fillers and fluff and replace them with something that's really important to you.

We live in a world where it seems increasingly difficult to find time, and to focus on what's really important to us, yet somehow we are able to busy ourselves with, and obsess over that which will be meaningless in just a few days or months. The more you are able to make yourself and your life a priority, the more others will to.

My own personal Monthly Planner is an excellent tool for this, available in the Book Bonuses. Download the PDF that I created for myself to keep me on track. It's one page, it's simple, and it works.

29: Making Tough Decisions

"Man improves himself as he follows his path; if he stands still, waiting to improve before he makes a decision, he'll never move."
-Paulo Coelho

One of the most common issues I run into with clients, personally and professionally, is that feeling of "being stuck". More often I find on closer examination, that it's really about how to make those tough decisions.

We all know this one; we've all been there. Dragging our feet on something or other when we think we know what we should do, but just can't seem to commit. There can be a whole process around decision making, particularly major life or business impacting decisions. This frequently involves gathering information, due diligence and weighing the facts. But there is another component that is often overlooked – the emotional component that can keep us feeling insecure, uncertain and ultimately unable to move. Here are some tips to help you develop the confidence and conviction you need in any situation to make your best decision.

Limit the number of small decisions you make at a time. In the last few years, scientists have documented a condition known as 'decision fatigue'. It's real, and clever advertisers and retailers know this and use it to their advantage, (limited time offers and the most expensive new car options saved until the end of the buying process.)

We are all bombarded with so much information on a daily basis that we are being asked to make small decisions all day long. Add in life challenges and financial limitations, and the decisions become exponentially more difficult, causing us to spend a disproportional amount of time deliberating over small things.

Notice when you are feeling mentally fatigued, when you have had to make too many small decisions in a short time period, and put off the major one until the next day when you can approach it with a clear mind. Schedule it in first thing, and especially before email, when your mind is clear and fresh.

Be clear about what is really important to you. Surprisingly, this is one of the toughest questions for many people to answer, "What makes you truly happy? What is deeply important to you?" We are so use to doing what other people expect of us, and what we think we should be doing, that we lose sight of, or never really figured out what would make us happy. Take some time and answer these questions:
What would you do if no one cared?
What would you do if no one else would ever find out?
What would you try if it didn't have to be perfect?
What would you do if you knew you couldn't fail?
Think about the times in your life that you were the happiest. What were you doing then? Now think of the most unhappy times? Compare the two and your life today. What can you change? And where are the gaps?

Hold off on the hot buttons. We all have things that set us off; things that evoke overly strong or disproportionate emotional reactions to the situation at hand. I call this your "inner terrorist" or the "emotional hot buttons".

Usually your "inner terrorist" is somewhere between the age of 4 and 14. It's that little voice in your head that stubbornly refuses to do something or other, or makes adamant demands about something else.

We are usually able to justify our choices, at least to ourselves, but these are the ones that leave you feeling really riled up, self righteous, scared or exhausted. This is the voice of your "inner terrorist" running your life.

Pay attention to what makes you hopping mad or really gets you going, and allow yourself a little time to calm down. Write out the details of the situation and ask yourself if you didn't know the person saying this, how old would you think they were? If it's starting to sound like an angry teenager, chances are it is. We've all been there too. Be gentle with yourself and that part of you that is so upset. Take some time, calm down and re-approach the situation.

What decisions, big or small have you been putting off? Where are you stuck and what do you need to clean up? Start to eliminate some of the small decisions and schedule in a time for the big ones. You'll feel lighter, freer and at this point forward movement will start to take care of itself.

Following the steps above, see if you can't get unstuck. If you're still having trouble after going through everything suggested, it may be the perfect time to hire a coach.

Part IV
Dealing With
The Outer World

30. Crystal Clear Communications

"The single biggest problem in communication is the illusion that it has taken place."
- **George Bernard Shaw**

One of the biggest issues I've seen in the years working with clients is that of communication. So often, situations can go array simply for lack of crystal clear communications. Part of the problem is also part of the beauty; we all have different communication styles, backgrounds and experiences that we're coming from. And as much as this adds to the inherent complexity and fascination of life, it can also be frustrating when we are "speaking different languages" and are not even aware of it.

A favorite example is from a client that I worked with several years ago. They would continually get into arguments with their partner over Sunday brunch. Both people loved leisurely Sunday mornings and a slow easy meal savoring time together. Both felt this was the perfect way to spend a late morning / early afternoon, and agreed that they wanted to do this together. So what's the problem? Why did Sunday brunch always result in a disagreement, hurt feelings and unnecessary drama? Because they hadn't taken the time to establish what "brunch" meant to each one of them individually; essentially to define the word.

In this particular situation, one person loved the casual atmosphere that Sundays brought in. Brunch meant you pulled on a pair of jeans, threw on a baseball cap and t-shirt and headed over to the local diner for an hour or two. Low commitment, low pressure.

The second person in this scenario enjoyed the formality involved with Sundays. Brunch was an event. It was something the family did together. You dressed for it and made reservations. It started with champagne cocktails and appetizers and allowed lengthy time for in-depth and enlivening conversations and connection. It could often consume the better part of the day, and wasn't to be rushed. Essentially, each person had a different picture in their minds for what "Sunday brunch" meant. They both had an entirely different expectation for the day. And both people, couldn't understand why the other one was being so unreasonable. They had simply come from different experiences and hadn't clarified this through communication. Once they gained some perspective, it brought with it more understanding. They were able to compromise with each other and take turns with the Sunday brunch experience.

From the outside it's easy to see how something so simple could go so wrong, but from inside the picture; and we're all inside the pictures in our own lives, things aren't always so obvious. Here are a few simple rules for crystal clear communications.

Get Clear. This may seem obvious, but easier said than done. Make sure, as in the example above that you both have the same idea of exactly what it is that you are talking about. If brunch can mean such different things to different people, imagine what different ideas there could be on love, marriage, relationships, office etiquette and more. Asking for clarification is not rude, nor does it mean you're a moron, is healthy and respectful for everyone involved and the relationships.

Drop the Defenses. If someone is truly trying to get clear with you, whether asking for more information or offering it, don't get huffy. This is not a personal affront or attack, it's only information. The same applies in reverse. As many opportunities as there are for getting offended, there are just as many for understanding. Ask first before making any hasty judgments.

Say What You Mean, and Mean What You Say. How many times have you taken someone's words to heart, only to have them say "I was only kidding." Or "I just said that. I didn't mean anything by it."
In a business situation this can be frustrating, time consuming and costly; in personal situations, heartbreaking. Speak your truth and stand by it. We don't get to keep many things in this life, but the value of your word can never be taken from you, only given away.

Listen. We all want to be heard, but the other half of that is listening. I can only be heard if you give me your attention and listen to me, and vice versa. Being heard feels great! And through listening we can learn so much. When someone is speaking, physically close your mouth; this actually increases your capacity to hear. Before you start formulating your response in your head, let them finish. Food is no good half-baked, and neither are our ideas or responses.

Respond, Respond, Respond. Communication is a two way street, and if listening is one half, responding is the other. Conversation, written or verbal is alive, it's an interchange. It's very much like throwing a ball and playing catch. My job is not only to toss the ball to you in a manner in which you are most likely to catch it, but to do my best to catch it - receive it, when you return it to me. Going silent, not acknowledging the other person's statements or questions or not confirming (as in the case of emails, voicemails etc.) can lead to misunderstandings, confusion and hurt feelings.

Once you have taken the time to listen, give the other person the gift of knowing they've been heard. This is also a great way to nip misinterpretations in the bud!
Life is all about communications. It starts with our first cry and finishes with our last breath. Every interchange with another person is, at its core, communication. So wouldn't it make sense for all of us to get really good at it?

I challenge you to get clearer with your communications. Pick one area from the list above and see if you can master it. Notice what changes it brings about in your life, how you interact with others and them with you?
Listen up, get clear, respond, and enjoy a new simplicity and alacrity in communications.

31. What To Do When "It's" Not Working

"Each time we rest in contentment, generate compassion, let go of attachment, we are moving beyond stress and confusion that keep us trapped in a short sighted view."
— ***Sakyong Miphram Earth Protector***

We've all experienced this at some point in our lives. We set a goal, we make big plans to achieve it, work really hard and still don't get the results we've been hoping for and desire! Maybe it's losing weight, growing our business, changing jobs or creating that perfect romantic relationship. Whatever it is that you're longing to accomplish or create, continually exerting the efforts without realizing the ideal results, can leave you feeling exhausted, frustrated and deeply disappointed.

One thing most of us fail to recognize is that when this happens undoubtedly our ego is involved. We don't want to admit that we've made a mistake; an error in judgment, and that what we're so caught up in doing isn't working and isn't going to! We continue to try to pound the round peg into the square hole hoping that by some miracle, this time it's going to fit! What we really need is new information, and redirection. The great Jim Rohn once said, "If a person is going down the wrong road, they don't need motivation to speed them up, they need education to turn them around!"

Here are a few simple steps to get yourself turned around, when the road you're on has been a path of frustration and is not in the direction of your dreams.

This may seem obvious, but Stop What You're Doing! So often in the grips of desperation we continue on pushing further, even when it's not working, and not getting us what we want. We're afraid that if we stop, it means that we're lazy, unmotivated, or worse yet, didn't really want "it" to begin with. Being deeply committed to a dream means allowing yourself the time to reevaluate and regroup, moving forward with clearer focus and better information.

Admit That You Don't Know. (I personally hate this one!) I love being right as much as the next person. Sometimes as a coach, I feel like I should have all the answers, but the truth and reality is from time to time we are all going to be in a position where we just don't know why something isn't working. We are going to bump up against lack of knowledge and inexperience every time we try to make a big change or grow. We have to. Which leads me to the next step…

Seek Outside Expert Advice. I have worked with some pretty phenomenal coaches over the years, and have witnessed time and again just how much easier my life can become when I take the time to seek outside expert advice or mentoring. If our dishwasher breaks down, most of us have no problem in calling in an expert, yet when it comes to our weight, our careers, our businesses, our lives, we feel like we have to go it alone. Give yourself the gift of a little support, and get the help of someone who does know what to do when you don't.

Protect Your Dream. Usually when we're deeply committed to pushing ahead in spite of unfavorable results, there is an emotional component to our desire. The success or failure in achieving it speaks of our abilities and defines our self-worth. This is the dominion of dreams. When seeking advice or help, be gentle with yourself and insist that others are too. Input should be constructive and creative, building on what's working, correcting what's not, and tearing down only what absolutely has to go.

For many of us, admitting that we don't know and seeking outside help can leave us feeling uncomfortable and vulnerable. Resist the urge to be defensive, or pretend to know more than you do. Bite your tongue and listen. Then sit with the new ideas and thoughts for a day or two and let them percolate.

If you're faced with an insurmountable problem, or stuck on a treadmill of unproductive action, stop, take time, breathe, and get some help. It may be all it takes to turn you around on the road from failure to fulfillment.

32. Dealing With Drama

"Gossip kills three: the speaker, the spoken of, and the listener."
- Samuel b. Nahman, Numbers Rabbah

One of my first coaches - a sharp, smart lady, had a few simple rules for running her business and her life. I learned to love these rules and quickly adopted them as my own: "Work Hard, Have Fun, No Drama."
But being human, every once in a while I slip, and last week I broke rule #3, "No Drama". What ensued was, life became less fun, and I got less work done, and all because of a little drama! Read on, and discover what I learned about personally dealing with drama.

Drama comes in many forms. It could show up as a bitter divorce, squabbling between family members, misunderstandings and legal hassles, or petty jealousies between friends. Sometimes we're even the source of our own drama; beating ourselves up for perceived mistakes, over-thinking issues, or worrying incessantly about things that are beyond our control.
Whatever the source, drama can take over your life, and drain your energy. While some things definitely take time to resolve, you'll be healthier and happier if you can do it, minus the drama.

Here is a quick check list to help you identify any areas of drama in your own life:

__ are you always talking about or thinking about a particular person or situation

__ do you feel an ongoing sense of emotional entanglement or dread

__ are you prone to gossiping, or discussing things that would be better left unsaid

__ do you often feel fed up, anxious or frustrated

__ is there one person in your life who seems to continually emotionally ignite everyone in your group or family

__ are there situations that you know you should deal with but haven't

__ is it difficult for you to be truthful with others involved in those situations

__ do you find yourself continually pulled into matters that have little or nothing to do with you

We are all caught up in drama at one time or another, but you certainly don't have to stay there! If you found yourself checking any of the items above, start by looking at steps you can take to begin to minimize some of the drama.

Stop talking about it. Catch yourself when you have the urge to gossip or rehash every little detail – this won't produce any more solutions, only more drama.

Be in impeccable integrity. When you are truthful with yourself and others about what's going on, drama has little roots to take hold. Tell the truth, avoid the drama.

Identify "hot spots". We all have them and know them. If certain people or places push your buttons, start by staying away. If this isn't possible, seek the help of an experienced professional to assist you in working through whatever it is that gets you so riled up. Whatever you do, don't endure it just hoping it will resolve itself.

Look for solutions. So often in life we are conditioned to look for what's wrong, focusing on the problem and not the solution. This only keeps you unhappy and stuck. Acknowledge the problem, but concentrate on the solution and then take consistent action to bring it into being.

Don't play ball. It takes two people or teams to have a game; don't be one of them. Do what you must to deal with the situation, but walk away from the drama. My personal motto: if this was a tennis match, put the racquet down. Stop lobbing the ball back and forth. You'll give yourself and problem the best chance for success and resolution.

So my next challenge to you is to deal with your drama. Identify where it is, look for solutions and take the steps to clean it up. Movies and books are great for drama; it's usually better thought out and still has a conclusion in the end, so enjoy it, and then leave it there.
Remember: Work Hard. Have Fun! No Drama.

33. Problems

"The good news is, there are going to be problems."
- **The Coach**

Every once in a while I have a bad day - a really bad day; so do clients I work with. But one of the things I've come to realize over the years, is that bad weeks, bad moods, and in the longer term, on-going depression, often results when we expect life to be free of problems.

Somehow, there seems to have been a big hiccup in the self-help industry. People have come to mistakenly believe that if you think good thoughts, meditate or pray and say positive affirmations, that all of life is going to be worry-free and wonderful. That's just not the case.

While positive thinking is an important piece of the puzzle, it's not the only piece. Sometimes it's going to rain on your birthday, the car will break down, you may get a red wine stain on your favorite shirt, miss a flight and the list goes on. In short, stuff happens! We can't control the entire universe. And do you really want to? A) That's an awfully big job, and I don't know about you, but I'm already a little busy. B) Problems are just surprises that we don't like. If you could control absolutely everything, think of all of the really neat surprises that you'd miss out on?

Problems are not only something that you didn't plan on and don't care for; they're a sign that something isn't working, that it needs your attention and needs to be better figured out.

True problems, (other than the whole raining on your birthday thing), are generally a sign of progress. Where there are no problems, there is no progress.

When your website crashes, you lose data on your computer, a major auto manufacturer is forced to do a large scale recall, or your darling little angel ends up in the principal's office or worse, it's all a sign that something needs to change.
You'll probably put stronger back-up systems in place that are going to serve you much better in the long run. The auto manufacturer is going to sink millions more into research and development and implement higher standards for automobile safety and production. And your little darling? Well, you know there is a life lesson just waiting to be served up there - probably for both of you :)

The first thing to know about problems is that they will come up, what's important is how you deal with them.

Anticipate the ones you can and plan your solutions in advance. Example: back up your computer regularly, and in multiple ways. You want to prepare for the worst and protect your data.

Realize that problems are the sign that something that is important to us; it means there is an underlying goal.
Example:
Problem: Your weight has been creeping up and you don't fit into half or your clothes anymore.
Goal: You'd like to be more physically fit and healthy, or at least look good in your wardrobe.

Know where there is a goal, there is always a (another) solution** More about this in the Homework Section below.

The Bigger the Problem, the Bigger the Goal. Example: back to the automobile manufacturer - Several years ago a major automobile manufacturer was forced to do a massive recall due to a safety issue. There was much media coverage and the company treated this very seriously, with the head of the company addressing it personally and very publicly. I went online to check out their company mission statement. Here is how it reads: "To attract and attain customers with high-valued products and services and the most satisfying ownership experience in America."

Considering how many millions of vehicles are sold in North America every year, "...the most satisfying ownership experience in America." is a massive goal. If they didn't care about their brand, their name, or the quality of their products, the problem would have simply been a matter of economics, and probably dealt with much more quietly.

I've been fortunate to work with some very successful clients over the years, and their lives are far from free of problems. In fact, the more successful they become, the bigger the problems, because they are continually increasing the size of their goals. The key difference I've noticed in what determines the degree of success is not the number of problems, but the ability to deal with them.

It's like lifting weights, you start with the little ones, and as you get stronger, you build up to the bigger ones. Problems are our way of building and flexing our life-skills muscles. As the saying goes, "Don't wish it was easier, wish you were bigger/better/stronger."

Coaching Homework: I'd like to challenge you to take a new look at your problems. Start by writing down three to five of biggest problems in your life right now. Then, write down the goal associated with the problem.

Once you've done that start brainstorming some possible action steps you could begin taking. You don't have to implement all of them, or even any of them, they are only POSSIBLE solutions. Be as creative as you can, and if you're having trouble with this, brainstorm with a friend, read up on it, or hire a coach. Once you've done that pick one action that you can take from your solutions list to start moving closer towards your goal.

Example:

Problem: I feel lonely and stuck

Goals: To have more friends, be in a relationship, have a great social life and move forward in my career

Possible Actions: Join an online dating service. Commit to getting out twice a week, (dance class, yoga, gym). Get involved with a local organization, Chamber of Commerce, etc. Commit to lunch or coffee with one new person per month. Polish up my resume. Make a list of possible career moves. Upgrade my skills.

If peace, balance and harmony is your goal, that's fairly easy to do while sitting in a warm sunny meadow, but the minute the meadow gets dark and windy, your clothes need washing, you're kind of lonely and you have nowhere to sleep, you suddenly have a problem. And do you really want to live without a house, clothing, modern conveniences and other people anyway? Well guess what, they all come with lots of great attributes but they also come with their own problems.

Some people say that "Problems are life's way of seeing how serious we are." Or a friend said to me recently, "There are problems or inconveniences. It's only a problem if it's immediately life threatening, otherwise it's an inconvenience." And by the way, he's a veterinarian. Take it from me, (who has been in tears in his office more than once) he knows a few things about what is life threatening, and solving problems.

So this week and this month, see if you can embrace a few of your problems. Look for the hidden goal in them, find some new solutions and move forward to a bigger and better life. And as you do, in time, as you become stronger, you'll look back on them as inconveniences, and it's some of these that really make life worth living!

34. Getting Back on Track

"If someone is going in the wrong direction, they don't need motivation to speed them up but direction to turn them around."
- Jim Rohn

There are certain times of the year that we are uber productive and highly motivated. Traditionally, September tends to be one of the busiest months of the year for people. The summer is over, vacations are behind us, and most of us are eager to move forward with new ideas and new plans.
New Years is another one of those times. Generally I find, the first couple of weeks tend to go fairly well; maybe hectic, but we are getting so much done and tend to be feeling very pleased with ourselves. But it's usually around this time that things begin to unravel. The break-neck pace catches up with us; little hiccups start to appear in what we thought to be flawless plans and family disagreements turn to disputes under the added pressure. So what do we do when we've been moving along so smoothly and suddenly everything starts to fall apart? Here are a few practical tips to help you get back on track.

"Nothing very, very good, or very, very bad, lasts for very, very long." This is one of my favorite sayings. It doesn't need much explanation, but sometimes it helps to remind ourselves of this. Whether you're at the top of your game, or at the bottom, this too shall pass. It always has before, and it will again.

Stop. When things are not going as we had planned, we often have the urge to push more, to try even harder, but if you're already going down the wrong road, the last thing you need is to pick-up speed. Just stop, maybe for a day or two. Reassess. It will give you some peace and the time to figure out whether or not you need to move in a different direction.

Have Fun! This may sound crazy, but boy does it work! You can't possibly think straight when the pressure is mounting and you are stressed out. Doing something fun, whatever that is for you, gives your brain a break, and you will come back with new and usually better ideas and insights.

Reassess. When things start to unravel (or have completely fallen apart!) and you have taken the time to stop and have a little fun, then it's time to reassess. Doing this methodically - writing things out; helps most of us to think more clearly. Ask yourself, A) "What exactly am I trying to achieve? B) By when? C) Why? D) What happened that I didn't foresee or expect? E) Given what I know now, what is a really good next step?"

Modify and Move On. Don't dwell on the failures. As the saying goes, "what you focus on expands," so focus on what you'd like to the outcome to be, rather than anything that's gone amiss along the way. And of course, take action. Act on that "really good next step". Action and accomplishment are the cures for disappointment and frustration.

If you find your world becoming a little chaotic, unraveled or things just aren't going as planned, take heart; know that you're not alone. Do what you can, where you are right now, and if you're truly at a loss for ideas, it may a good time to hire a coach. Either way, step by step, with some patience, and perseverance, things will begin to change.

35. Are You Using All of Your Resources?

"When every physical and mental resource is focused, one's power to solve a problem multiplies tremendously."
- ***Norman Vincent Peale***

As human beings, you only have to take a quick look around to see how we handle our precious resources. We squander them, waste them and take them for granted, always expecting life (and the planet) to deliver up more. But do we really handle things so differently in our personal lives? Aren't our homes just a microcosm of what we're creating in the world around us; the macrocosm? So, are you squandering your resources?

Let me back up just a bit, so what are resources? What's the first thing that comes to your mind? Electricity? Fuels? Fresh water? Those are the obvious ones, but resources go well beyond that.

Webster's defines resources as: 'a stock or supply of money, materials, staff, and other assets that can be drawn on by a person or organization in order to function effectively'. So now, specifically, what are your resources? Resources may be people you know, the supplies you have in your utility cupboard, food that's in the fridge or pantry, of course money, lines of credit, even clothing, shoes and office supplies. These are all resources.

How effectively and efficiently are you using yours? Are you using them up completely, and enjoying them in the process? Or do things get thrown out, forgotten, or collect dust in the closet or cupboard? Do you listen to all of the CD's you buy? Read all of the books, and complete all of the classes or programs? And what about that gym or health club memberships, or other monthly subscriptions?

Here's an example from my own life; for months now, I've been experiencing back pain. I've stretched, exercised, seen chiropractors and massage therapists. I changed my desk and my office chair, tried to relax more and stress less. I had done just about everything I could think of that was at my disposal at the present time. But after months of suffering, in an hour of desperation, I sat down and asked myself "Is there anything that I'm not doing that I could be?"

What came to mind was an unused resource. Now I'm in the hot tub regularly - almost daily, and in combination with the other efforts, pleased to say that the pain has subsided significantly; thanks to a little discipline and determination and fully using my resources.

I had to first overcome my own ideas that 'it wouldn't make that big of a difference' or that 'I didn't have enough time during busy workdays' as well as a few other arguments I had concocted for myself to avoid taking action. I now see this to be a valuable resource.

So what resources do you have in your life that you're not using fully? Are there people that could help you? Is there a book on the shelf that you know you should read? Candles that you never burn? Supplements or skincare products that go unused because they take a little extra effort and time every day? Or maybe guided meditations you haven't listened to in months that soothe frazzled nerves? Perhaps even a bicycle that seldom sees the outside of the garage? When you think of things in these terms, can you see how rich your life is with resources? And are there any that you are no longer using that you could donate or pass on to someone else?

Fully using, enjoying and caring for all of our resources is a way to care for ourselves and the planet as well. It brings in to awareness the enormous abundance we have in our lives and how fortunate we are to live in this beautiful country.
And the more we utilize and appreciate the resources we already have, the more the universe is inclined to put at our disposal. So this week, why not take a look around your own little microcosm; your own life, and look for unused resources. Care for them, cherish them, use them and enjoy them, fully and completely and watch as the universe seemingly miraculously delivers more!
We're all in this together on this planet, and "how you do anything is how you do everything." So how would you like to see the world handle precious resources?

Part V
Show Me The Money

36. Uncovering Your Hidden Money Story

"Our first duty is not to be poor.
Don't be part of the problem."
- **George Bernard Shaw**

Money is seldom a neutral subject in today's society. Whether you are earning more than enough to support your lifestyle wants and needs or barely making ends meet, chances are that you have an emotional charge around money.

In our society money is power. It ensures that you have a safe comfortable place to live, enough high quality food to eat, access to medical care, comfortable and beautiful clothing and your children are well educated and provided for. And these are just the basics.

There has long been the argument that 'money can't buy love,' and it's not suppose to! But it touches everything you do love. Because of this, few things can deplete your energy, your passion and your sex drive more quickly than struggles and stresses around money. But how do you really feel about money? What is your unconscious money story? And how is it impacting, or even ruling your life?

In his book, *Secrets of the Millionaire Mind*, T. Harv Eker refers to it as our "financial blueprint". Just as our homes and offices are built from a plan, so are our lives - our relationships, our health and our finances. The difference is that the original blueprint for our lives was not one of our own making. It was drafted by the ideas, morals, values and lifestyle choices of our families, and the society in which we were raised.

As we mature, slowly we start to take ownership of this plan, and adapt it to fit our current needs, ideas and experiences. But the big flaw with this blueprint is that it's written in invisible ink, so we stumble into hidden walls, trip over obstacles and the odd time unwittingly knock out a crucial support. So what does your financial blueprint really look like? Just look around your life. Is it small and cramped? Or spacious and luxurious? Is it complicated and troublesome? Or is it clear and simple? To help you uncover your hidden financial blueprint, I've put together a few questions. Taking the time to answer these (about 15 minutes) is like the old scout trick with lemon juice on paper - turning up the heat on the invisible ink suddenly makes it easy to read.

1. What is your money personal story? What would you tell a complete stranger about your financial life to date?
2. What is your family money story? What ideas about money were you raised with?
3. How do you handle money? Do you have too much, too little, or never enough? Do you hoard it, waste it, ignore it? Do you have enough for your future or are you hoping it will all turn out okay?
4. What are the emotions you have around money?
How would you prefer to feel about money?
When it's time to pay bills, how do you feel? What thoughts run through your head?
5. Complete this sentence in as many ways as you can: Money is….
6. If you were casting the role of money for a movie, who would play the part of Money?
7. Do you have any shame around money? (Having more than family members? Less than co-workers? Carrying debt?)

8. How much money would be enough so that you could feel secure and never had to work again?

The abundance of or lack of money impacts the way you see yourself, others and the world. It can affect your health and vitality, your body, your relationships and your work and career. It's a highly charged issue that crosses cultures, generations and continents. So why not take some time this week and look at your "money blueprint". Decide if it's one you like, or if it's time to tear down some walls and build something new.

37. Escaping the Credit Epidemic

"People often overestimate what will happen in the next two years and underestimate what will happen in ten."
- **Bill Gates**

We don't need to look too far to see signs of mounting credit problems in our society today. Not only is it the focus of every newscast and headline, it has impacted our families, our friends, our communities, and for many, our personal lives. We are constantly reminded of the "credit crunch" and the heavy mountains of debt that so many find themselves struggling under. But what has led us to such a point, and more importantly how do we regain our strength and recover? The answer, while simple, is not easy or quick. Easy and quick is what got us into this mess in the first place. It's that desire to "turn a blind eye" or "worry about it tomorrow" that has finally caught up with us and is demanding our attention – with considerable interest.

But our credit woes are not just limited to our finances. They are pervasive in every area of our lives. We indulge in sweets, alcohol, rich foods and drugs, skipping the gym, and hope that our health will hold out a little longer. We work long hours, neglecting our family, friends and recreation, trusting that there will be time tomorrow for all of them, and that those closest to us will still be there, waiting. We put off going for our amazing lives, great careers and soulful relationships, because there is always one more thing to do first. We suck ourselves in with the illusion that there are endless tomorrows;

there aren't. We live our lives constantly opting for short term gratification instead of long term fulfillment, and this is the treacherous trap of credit.

So how pervasive is "credit buying" in your life? Where are you robbing your tomorrows to pay for today? And are you willing to take the necessary steps to stop? Below are a few ways to help you identify the deficits in your life, and some simple guidelines for turning them around.

• Are you constantly tired and in need of sleep, or running on caffeine, promising yourself that you'll "catch up" on it tomorrow?

• Do you have a health problem that you've been neglecting, or have you put on weight, that you'll deal with when you have a little more time and less stress?

• Are you over spending, in anticipation that "next month or next year will be better"?

• Do you have adequate retirement savings, or are you hoping that it will somehow all work out?

• Are you in a relationship that's "good for now" but ultimately not one that you see yourself in long term?

• Are you in a job that pays the bills but will never create the dream you have for your life, and with no exit plan?

• Do you procrastinate on your work, favoring video games or TV, having to run frantic and stressed later to make up for what should have already been done?

• Is there a void in your life due to lack of support from close friends or in your primary relationship that you are ignoring or haven't dealt with? And what are the long term effects?

These are the ways that we rip ourselves off with short term feel goods, or even doing what's easier in the moment, instead of doing what's right for long term happiness in our lives. We spend time, money and energy that we don't have, telling ourselves that if we just take care of today, we can worry about the rest tomorrow. And *worrying* about it tomorrow is exactly what we are doing. Except tomorrow has become today, and the worry is now.

As I said earlier, the solution is simple, but perhaps not easy or quick. (If it was, we'd already be doing that instead!) The only way we can stop cheating our tomorrows, is by living within the reality of today – even when that reality isn't pretty or doesn't feel good in the short term. When we live in the truth of the moment, we reconnect ourselves with our own power, giving ourselves the strength and permission to move forward in a more healthy and grounded way.

Coaching Exercise:

Take a gentle, honest look at your life; where are you at today? And are you robbing your future of its health, its wealth and it's joy? Answer the questions above, and see where you're "overspending".

Then make a list what needs to change to bring you back into alignment and integrity for a healthy, happy future.

Make a plan to start implementing the changes, slowly, and one at a time. If you don't know how to implement the changes, seek out experts to help you; a financial planner, trainer, a counselor or a coach.

Today will become tomorrow soon enough, in only a few hours as a matter of fact. And when you think of it being that close, doesn't it make sense to change?

38. Financial Self Esteem

"Too many people spend money they haven't earned,
to buy things they don't want,
to impress people they don't like."
*- **Will Smith***

When financial planner and motivational speaker Suze Orman talks, people listen. Orman says we all need to get our financial priorities straight. *"The correct order is people, money and things. You have to care about yourself and others [first]. And you can't go from people to things; you need the money. You can't jump a chasm in two leaps. That's exactly what we tried to do and look what happened."*

Many times when I see people with financial worries, the order of their priorities is reversed; they are surrounded with things. Things they don't need, don't use, and sometimes aren't even that fond of. They end up with a lot of things in their house and in their life, instead of a lot of money in their bank accounts. At some point they've decided to value quantities of things over quantities of cash, leaving last on the list people - and namely themselves.

But here is where it gets tricky, when we truly value people, we must start with valuing ourselves first. If we sincerely valued ourselves above all else, would we really feel the need for the things? If we honored ourselves and our money, would we have the courage to forgo the new jewelry, trinkets or clothing, while paying off credit card debt? Or to drive an older car to take care of our retirement and long term financial health? If we had impeccable self-esteem, could we easily take care of ourselves and our money first, and then go for the things?

As with everything in life it's a cyclical process; the more we take care of ourselves, the more it raises our self-esteem. And the more self-esteem we possess, the more we are inclined to care for ourselves. So what can you do this week and this month to care for yourself and raise your financial self-esteem? Pick one small step, something you can do every day for at least two weeks to take care of yourself and your money, (letting go of things).

Could you...
- Stop impulse purchasing for two weeks.
- Give yourself the rest you need instead of the evening out you don't.
- Clean up any old financial issues – bills, paperwork, taxes. Spend 5 minutes a day reviewing your finances – even the parts you'd rather not look at.
- Track everything you spend - including household expenses and groceries, so you know exactly where your money is going (wouldn't you afford this much attention to a young child; our money needs the same amount of care).
- Get clear on your fixed and variable expenses, and create a savings plan and a separate "fun account" for more a little cushion in the future.

Another little trick I love, and try this as an experiment for two weeks; before you go into ANY store, decide first what you are going to buy. Leave the store with those items only and nothing else. You'll be surprised at just how much impulse purchasing you really do!

The correlation between debt and self esteem is not a new one. When our personal reserves are depleted, the finances are quick to follow. So this week, and this month, take really good care of yourself, and your money. It not only feels good, but the benefits are immediate, tangible, long lasting and far reaching.

39. Mastering Money

"Money frees you from doing things you dislike. Since I dislike doing nearly everything, money is handy."
Groucho Marx

Money is a topic that seems to come up a lot in coaching. As I mentioned in an earlier coaching tip, it's never neutral – there is always a high emotional charge around it. It's a subject that holds endless fascination or frustration for just about everyone.

Money is something that most people don't feel they have enough of; a few people feel they have too much of, and just about everyone is continually looking for a new way to manipulate, handle, save, invest or grow what they have. But how many of us have actually made a commitment to master the art and the skill of the subject of money?

It's said that it takes approximately 10,000 hours to master any specific task or subject. That's roughly 5 years of full time work, (assuming a 40 hour work week and 50 working weeks a year).

The actual time is assumed to be closer to 7 years, allowing for time off, set-backs and actions taken with lack of guidance. So how much time have you applied to mastering money? And specifically, your own? Is it something you enjoy dealing with? Are you good at it? Do you look forward to it? Or do you put it off? Do you take charge of your money, handling it and controlling where it goes? Giving it as much attention and direction as you would with a young child, new pet, or even a creeping vine.

Money is something we tend to worry about, fret about and fuss about, as if any of this was going to do any good. We trick ourselves into believing that all of that internal debate and commotion is productive action and that is somehow going to magically make things work out. It's this kind of self-deception and delusion that keeps us stuck in old patterns, and prevents us from moving ahead, achieving our financial goals and living our dreams. So my question to you is, are you ready to master money?

Think for a moment; what is something else in your life that you are really good at? Perhaps have even mastered? What is something that you enjoy doing because you are so good at it? What is something you could actually teach to someone else because you are exceptionally good at it? How long and what did it take for you to get really good at this particular thing? And are you willing to become even half that good at dealing with money?

To Master Money requires that we get really good at four key things:

Making Money. Creating more of it when you want it

Managing Money. Having systems in place to track it and control where it goes

Accumulating Money. Keeping some of what's coming in so you have a cushion

Using Money. To make your life easier and better (isn't that what it's meant for anyway?)

On a scale of 1-10 how would you rate yourself and your skills in each of those four areas? Can you see how they are all intrinsically tied to one another, interdependent? Take 5 minutes, and make a list of at least 2 things you could do in each area to improve your score in that sector and your skills of money mastery.

Here are a few suggestions for you to get you started:
• Review your own personal accounts and spending patterns.
• Revise your monthly budget.
• Read a book on money management.
• Consult with a financial planner.
• Begin a savings or investing plan.
• Take a course involving finances and/or investing.
• Brainstorm ways to create or bring in more money.
• Get clear on what you have, and nurture that.
• Get clear on what you want, and how you're going to get it.

Do you need more planning around money? More education? More information? Mastering money is no more mystical and mysterious than mastering anything else – it's a skill, nothing more. What typically holds us back is fear and lack of knowledge. If money is a concern for you, and if you're still reading, chances are it is, do yourself a favor and take one small step closer to mastering your money. You'll be glad you did.

40. Money as a Spiritual Path

"A big part of financial freedom is having your heart and mind free from worry about the what-ifs of life."
- **Suze Orman**

Money is not often thought of as a "spiritual path". In fact, just the opposite. Notice what your own instantaneous reaction to this is. What kind of people make and have a lot of money? What kind of people are deeply spiritual? And are they the same? If your initial response is not a whole-hearted yes, or even a maybe, there could be an opportunity here for a little spiritual financial healing to take place.

If you and I were to have a completely candid conversation right now about your finances; how you handle money, earn money, save money, spend money and invest money, what would your first emotional response be? Would it be one of enjoyment, anticipation, relief? Or would it be something a little less comfortable? Often times I find the first reaction is one of guilt, shame and embarrassment, so if this is you, or anything similar, take heart – you're not alone.

Much of the new age thinking tells us that if we really loved ourselves we'd have more money, or an abundance of money. That's only true if you have the desire PLUS the understanding, knowledge, know-how, tools and support to create it. There is skill involved in this. We all know mean, unloving people with a lot of money, and we know kind generous people who have very little money. The opposite also holds true.

Wealthy patrons are often counted on by community organizations to support hospitals, libraries, social projects and the arts – far from being ungiving, And Warren Buffet as the quintessential example has personally donated billions – yes, that's with a 'b' to charities.

I always say that "situations don't make people, they reveal them". The same holds true for money. It acts as a magnifier for what is already going on in your life. But know that it's just that – an indicator, nothing more. Just as your car lets you know when it's time to add more fuel, your financial picture lets you know where your strengths are and what needs more attention.

Which brings me back to spirituality. Money, if that's a stuck point for us, also symbolizes our next point of spiritual breakthrough. Go back to your emotions around money and finances, and take a few minutes to jot down your feelings around these:

• How do you feel about handling your money?
• Are you meticulous and careful in your spending, or try not to think about where it goes?
• Do you enjoy managing your finances?
• What about investing?
• When you think of having to create more money, what is the first emotion that comes up?
• If I asked you to list 3 general feelings toward money what would they be?

If you already have all of the money you want and need, can create it on demand, hold on to what you create, and are completely content, there will be no energy here. But if not, then these are exactly the spiritual and emotional blocks that you will be forced to confront in order to bring more money into your life. Some of the most common are: denial, anger, mistrust, shame, embarrassment, a feeling of incompetence, guilt and issues around what you feel you deserve. But what are the key emotions for you? And where else is this showing up in your life?

What we don't want to do here is to focus on the problem. Never let the diagnosis become the prognosis. Remember, it's simply an indicator. In other words, I don't want to hear "Oh well, I'll never have much money… it's my low self esteem issues," or "I just feel so guilty asking for money for what I do! I could never do that!" Yes, notice it, be aware of it, and then make a decision to work through it. And this is the spiritual path. In this respect, money can be the ultimate healer. As we commit to getting our financial life in order, to earn what we deserve, save and invest wisely and pay down our debt, we heal the shame and frustration and other negative emotions as well as boosting our confidence in our abilities and our self-esteem.

Make a commitment to heal whatever it is that is holding you back; don't just give in to it. Be gentle with yourself, but firm – don't back down. This is going to get uncomfortable, but that's just part of the process.

Recently I was working with a client who had continually in her life gone through cycles of "feast and famine". For a while, she would make a lot of money, have good solid investments, buy beautiful things and be completely debt free. But then, inevitably there would be a crash. Some kind of life disaster would eat up all of the savings, there would be a job loss, move or other circumstance that would result in steadily declining income, or no income at all. And before you know it she was starting all over again. By doing the exercise above, she was able to realize that once she had money, she felt that everyone would want it from her, and rather than dealing with the responsibility of setting healthy money boundaries, she unconsciously sabotaged her best efforts.

Once she approached money as a spiritual path, she was able to find the courage to take on the uncomfortable adult behavior of deciding who she would help, with how much and when - and not feel guilty about any of it. Her income steadily increased as she stepped through the fear and into her own money power. She not only had more money to help people close to her and give to charities, but she was also able to keep much more for herself without feelings of guilt or as she put it "being miserly". She now sees herself as a brave, empowered woman around money, and not always the shrinking adolescent.

Living with money problems is like living with any other problem long term; it depletes our energies, robs us of vitality and keeps us stuck and playing small. This week, make a list of 3-5 things that you need to do to start creating a healthier financial future, and by all mean, get extra help with this if you need to. As you start to take charge of your finances, watch as your spirit soars!

Part VI
Taking Care of YOU

41. Extreme Self Care

"When your body mind and soul are healthy and harmonious, You will bring health and harmony to those around you and health and harmony to the world not by withdrawing from the world but by being a healthy living organ of the body of humanity."
- **B.K.S. Iyengar**

We all experience stress in our lives at one time or another, and sometimes it can seem absolutely overwhelming. When this happens, we tend to run ourselves ragged; lose sleep and worry endlessly, hoping that if we feel bad enough, somehow the tides will turn and miraculously improve the situation. We often ignore our health, and diminish our well-being, when what would serve us best is increased self care.

When I mention self-care, what's the first image that comes to your mind? Is it one of relaxing on a beach or at a spa, or indulging in a long lazy day off? And notice what your feelings are around this? For most of us this little fantasy is pleasure mixed with guilt. We tend to thrive on hectic, overcrowded schedules that we love to divulge to anyone who will listen. We wear them like a badge of honor, proud of our exhaustion and the accompanying stress. This is the proof that we are hard-working, selfless people. But unless we're striving to be martyrs or saints, where does this really get us?

Stress as the precursor to heart disease, diabetes, depression and other serious illness is not a new idea. So why don't we simply slow down? Why do we continually permit our days to fly by at break-neck speed with diminishing regard for the long term effects, or even our immediate enjoyment? Simple. Because we're not thinking clearly.

Our hectic, worrying and nerve-racking days produce a flood of stress chemicals in our brains. Immediately our system switches into crisis mode, the fight or flight response kicks in, reasoning ability recedes and then we wonder why our effectiveness and efficiency take a steep decline. This is the downward spiral of stress. And the remedy? Simple Self Care. Self Care is more than the occasional indulgence or guilty pleasure. It is the ongoing maintenance of our energy, the support of our vital life force and ultimately the foundation of our well being. It is the one thing that can turn your life around, when you feel like you've tried everything else. Here are a few tips to help you practice Extreme Self Care.

Trim your schedule of activities that you don't find deeply rewarding. If you feel like there are never enough hours in the day, then chances are you're spending too much time on things you just don't love or aren't that important. Tell yourself "that there is exactly enough time in the day to do whatever needs to be done." If it didn't get done, and nobody died as a result, then chances are, it didn't "need" doing.

What gives you more energy? Do you need to get more sleep? Would you be calmer if you meditated more? Are you getting enough exercise, fresh air, time with friends, pets, family, or just by yourself? Ask yourself what it is that really adds to your life force, and your own personal vitality, and then schedule in time for that daily – no matter what. You'll quickly see that this time is well-invested, not just spent, and the dividends are huge.

Make caring for yourself a priority. Remind yourself of the benefits of self-care, not the martyrdom of self-exhaustion. Truly caring for yourself will leave you feeling renewed and refreshed, clear and focused. You'll find you have more creative energy and more time to carry out other tasks.
So take some time and indulge in self care. Ask yourself what you could do for you on a daily basis? What is going to make you feel great, revitalized and cared for? What actions would you take if caring for a dear friend, loved one or small child? And now lavish this care upon yourself.

Self Care though simple, can yield significant results. You'll look and feel more vibrant and younger. Your time will seem to expand and effectiveness increase. As you feel lighter and more cared for your self-worth will skyrocket. And all this while doing things that are good for you, and feel good too! Even when schedules can be hectic, and life especially demanding, I invite you to practice unshakable Self Care. Commit to taking time for yourself daily, and eventually it will become routine and habit.

42. Surviving Stress

"Stress, in addition to being itself and the result of itself, is also the cause of itself."
- **Hans Selye**

Stress. It happens to everyone at some time or another. We get stressed about our work, our relationships, our finances, kids, health and homes. I've yet to meet anyone who leads a completely charmed life and never experiences any stress. However, in the last six months, I've seen the stress levels in clients, friends and business associates escalate to new heights. I don't need to point at current economic conditions or the global economy as a common denominator; this is not "news" to so many who have experienced the direct effects first hand. But the question is what do we do about it? What do we say to a friend or a loved one who is going through an especially tough time? What do we say to ourselves in the darkness of the night when mounting insecurities creep in? How do we unwind, stay focused and keep going… and maybe even relax and have a little fun along the way? The bad news is that it does take a little bit of focused effort. The good news is, it's easier than you think.

The first thing I encourage clients to do is to take a little break. Give yourself some breathing room, some space to step back and gain a clearer and broader perspective. This may be an afternoon, or better yet a weekend off, and just "let the problem go." Whatever it is that has got you so worried, will more than likely wait a couple of days. Put it out of your mind, but resolve to come back to it at a set day and time.

Once you've had some time off, come back to the current issue at hand, calmly, and with the intention of gaining more clarity and focus. Book some time for yourself (an hour or more) to sit down and look at all of the facts with a cool head, and clear mind.

If the issue is financial, how much? How much money/assets do you have? How much do you owe? How long could you continue with your current course of action without dire consequences? And what could you do today, right now, to improve the situation?

If relationships, health or family are the issue, apply the same process. What is really and truly going on? How do you feel about it? Is the current course of action going to serve you in the long term, or do you need to make a change? And what can you do today to improve the situation?

With a clearer view, and a bit of breathing room behind you, it's time to make a plan and take action! Focused action is always the remedy for worry and stress. It allows you to take back some control, instead of letting the situation control you.

So my challenge to you is to give yourself a break, make a plan and take action. Decide what it is that is most important to you right now, and what is the next step? Are there loose ends that need to be tied up, or papers and clutter to deal with? Is there something that you're avoiding doing because it's unpleasant or uncomfortable? Are you taking really good care of yourself right now – getting enough exercise, and sleep and eating healthy and nutritious foods?

During times of stress, it's more important than ever to focus on maintaining a balanced life, and protecting our health. Do you need to let a few things go, have some fun, and give yourself a break? Or is it time for you to get some outside help to deal with something that is beyond your scope of knowledge?

Stress and overwhelm are the result of feeling like we have no control over a given situation. When we feel like we have no options, we can quickly fall into anger, resignation and depression. While we can't always control what life brings our way, we can choose how we are going to deal with it. Some choices are tougher than others, but we always have choice. The first step towards the solution of any problem is optimism. Take heart, this too shall pass, but in the meantime, get clear, be good to yourself, and take action.

The fabulous Tina Turner said: "Sometimes you've got to let everything go – purge yourself. If you are unhappy with anything – whatever is bringing you down, get rid of it. Because you'll find that when you're free, your true creativity, your true self comes out."

43. Taking The Pressure Off

"Expect to have hope rekindled. Expect your prayers to be answered in wondrous ways. The dry seasons in life do not last. The spring rains will come again."
Sarah Ban Breathnach

If you're feeling extra pressured these days, it really is no wonder. The world actually is moving just a little faster and growing at an exponential rate.

The internet, that was non-existent in 1960, is now home to more that 300 million websites, and according to Google, approximately 50 billion individual web pages at the time of this writing. The world population? A mere 1 billion people in the year 1800. Now we top 7 billion; a staggering rate of growth. But how does this affect you personally?

A common issue that I see with clients, is that they feel like they are under constant pressure and there seems to be no relief in sight. People point to factors like "the economic crisis", mounting world tensions, global uncertainly, higher expectations at work, increased family pressures, and a constant barrage of emails and list of things "To Do" that seems to never end. If you can see even shades of this in your own life, take heart; you're not alone. But the question is what to do about it?

The thing I love about coaching is breaking issues down into practical, useful do-able steps; dealing with what you can, from where you're at and leaving (at least for now) the rest. What follows are a few simple tips to help you relieve some of the pressures in your own life.

What is it? Take just 5 minutes, and make a list of all the things that are currently stressing you out and creating more pressure in your life. It could be some of the things that I mentioned above, but I'd encourage you to be as specific as you can. If it's a global issue, how does this relate to your own life? Is it having a physical impact, or is it more mental and emotional? If work is a big pressure, again specifically what or who? Is there a person or a situation that is uncomfortable to deal with? Is it the type of work? Your salary? The commute? What is it exactly? And if home life is an issue, again what specifically about it? Be sure to include EVERYTHING on this list; no item is too small if it's causing you stress or discomfort.

Narrowing the field. Now that you have the big, broad list, look for the three biggies. What are the top three stressors on your list? Make sure that each of them is something that you can potentially exert some control over. i.e. If the fact that the world population has hit 7 billion is a stressful thought to you, you might want to let that go just for today unless you have a real concrete idea of what to do about it, and a reason why you should. Next put a mark beside the 3 items that are the easiest to fix. This may be things like cleaning out your inbox, organizing a closet, hanging a few pictures, making a dreaded phone call, or organizing your monthly finances.

Start small. There's an old expression, "nothing happens until something moves", so yes, the next step is to get moving. If needed, forfeit that Sunday night movie, or put off that dinner with friends, and just get a couple of these items out of the way and off your mind. Once you start relieving a little bit of the pressure, it'll give you clearer vision and insight into the remaining situations, allow you to act more succinctly, and hey... it just feels good! And isn't that what this is all about?

44. Letting Go and Moving On

"Experience is that marvelous thing that enables you to recognize a mistake when you make it again."
- Franklin P. Jones

For many of us as children, the word "forgiveness" was a daily part of our upbringing. We were told to turn the other cheek, and to forgive and forget. But more often than not, those instructions only applied to other people – many of whom wanted forgiving. I don't often recall being told to forgive myself, or even being presented with the idea that it was okay to do so.

Family members unwittingly brought up past embarrassments and indiscretions as fodder at Sunday dinner, and we relived the moment again and again. With that, also came the reliving of the criticism or punishment. It got replayed and engrained until it became part of our story. Where in there is there any forgiveness? And if we're not taught to forgive ourselves, where do we learn it?

As kids, we were constantly reminded of our mistakes, by people who were being constantly reminded of theirs. As adults, the pattern repeats itself. Most of us have stories that go something like this: "I should have taken better care of myself and my finances. I should have stayed married. I should have put more money in saving. I shouldn't have quit my job, bought the new car or moved house. I should never have trusted him/her. How could I be so blind? How could I be so stupid? Why did I not know better? I can't believe I'm going through this again."

In essence, we're running the same bad movie over and over again in our own heads. Our brains like to do this because it hates an unsolved problem; it/we are actually searching for and hoping for a better outcome or at least new take on the situation – one that we seldom get. But running that little horror flick keeps us stuck in self punishment and self blame. It depletes our energy, attacks our self-confidence and self-esteem and makes it more difficult to create new successes ahead. The remedy? You guessed it: forgiveness.

I'm surprised at how many people put up resistance to the idea of forgiving themselves. We seem to have an internal notion that self-punishment means that we're "good people" – after all, what kind of person would do what we have done and not feel guilt and remorse? Forgiveness doesn't mean absolving ourselves of responsibility, and it's not a free pass to repeat the action in question again. It simply means acknowledging our humanness and vulnerability, and creates space for learning and healing to begin.

As a coach, I've helped many clients, as well as myself, find self-forgiveness by asking the following questions:
- Were you in complete control of the situation, and could you have 100% guaranteed a different outcome?
- Given your skills and your knowledge at the time, were you really and truly in the position to make a different choice?
- Did you have the unconditional loving support of people around you?
- What greater need was being fulfilled at the time?

Make a list of things you need to forgive yourself for. What are

141

you tired of carrying and finally ready to put down? Here are a few to get you started that a client recently shared with me.

I forgive myself for…
• Staying in a relationship long after I knew it was over.
• Not saving more money or investing more wisely.
• Getting into debt.
• Saying something I know was going to be hurtful.
• Not calling _____more often.
• Not taking better care of myself, my health and my life.
• Acting in a way that was in conflict with my values or personal integrity.
• "Turning a blind eye" or "Not seeing it coming."

Most of us are doing the best we can, with the resources and knowledge we possess at any given moment. Understanding and learning from our mistakes is crucial to consistently moving forward, but so is forgiving ourselves for what we did, even when at times we may have known better. So, please, show yourself a little kindness. Get in touch with that small, scared part deep inside, and unconditionally give yourself the gift of forgiveness. You are sure to melt the bonds of your past, and be on your way to a brighter future.
See that any time you feel pained or defeated; it is only because you insist on clinging to what doesn't work. I love to refer to this quote when I find myself hanging on to something I suspect is no longer serving me;

"Dare to let go and you won't lose a thing
except for a punishing idea."
– Guy Finley, Author of The Secret of Letting Go

45. Getting Complete

"How does a project get to be a year behind schedule? One day at a time."
- **Fred Brooks**

So you have plans – big plans for this year, and maybe next! And for a while, things were just rockin' along. Then, slowly, you notice you're sitting at the computer dazed – staring at dozens of emails, 4 or 5 documents open on your desk top, even more browser windows going and the Smartphone sits and buzzes away next to you with texts, Twitter and Facebook messages waiting to be answered.

Now throw in a few phone calls, staff/family/colleagues wanting your attention and you can't concentrate or seem to get much of anything done. Does this sound familiar? If it does, know that you're not alone.

In today's fast-paced, high-tech, instant-download world, this is easy to do. We've come to view life as more of an "emergency" rather than something to be lived, built, created and enjoyed. We are bombarded with media telling us that we are lazy, or woefully behind the times if we don't do everything now. And surely we'll be doomed to failure for even a momentary lapse in attention to the latest trends. This, in my experience, just isn't so.

While I'm completely in favor of staying current, informed, in-touch and on top of your game; trying to do it all, all the time is a sure road to overwhelm. Essentially, we get nothing more than "information indigestion". We're simply not able to process everything that comes at us, at the speed it comes in.

When this happens, our brilliant brains take a little time out, leaving us staring blankly at mountains of emails, files, sticky notes, and other things that "need to get done". As the stress chemicals in our bodies build from the ensuing overwhelm we go into survival mode: fight, flight or freeze.

In fight mode, we may notice that we are just feeling an overall, un-point-at-able anger. We may start to become more abrasive with partners or colleagues or a little more short-tempered with service workers, family members and kids. We have a greater degree of adrenalin than usual and just want to vent!

In flight mode, we just want out – now! We've had enough, we need a vacation, this was a stupid idea anyway, we're going to change jobs/get a real job, hire some help or quit; anything to stop feeling the way we're feeling. This is also a prime time when we tend to indulge more in late-night movie watching, have an extra cocktail or two… or three, or maybe even dabble with drugs.

And next comes the big freeze. This is where we seem paralyzed to move forward. We know what should be done, (and boy is there a lot to do!) but we just can't seem to get a handle on it. Where do we start? The piles of papers? The emails? Or the dozen or so articles, apps, classes and other things that we want to check out that really might improve our lives, grow our businesses or further our careers?

The good news is that anything there is a way into, there is always a way out of, and in this case it begins with getting complete.

1. JUST STOP! Yes, that's right, stop in your tracks. Give yourself permission to "just be". (Remember: we're human be-ings, not human do-ings) Allow yourself some time to sit down and just let it all go, and reassess. This may be 30 minutes or even a whole day, depending on when the last time was you took a full day off. This is when you are going to formulate your plan of action for Step 2:

2. Next, it's time to get complete. Make a pact with yourself that for one or two days, nothing new gets dealt with, started or explored until you've completed everything that's currently open on your desk top. If there's a big backlog, you may have to space this out over a week, to continue to process the day to day realities of life and work.

3. Stop wandering down the rabbit hole. If you've ever gone online to post a quick tweet or look something up and suddenly realized that 2 hours have gone by, you know what I mean by this! This can be a fun, interesting, informative, and even inspirational or creative way to spend time, but it's also a clever way to avoid the not-so-fun tasks at hand. When you find something really interesting you'd like to explore further, make a note of it and come back to it at a later time. A really great idea is to allow 30-60 minutes for this at the end of the day. It keeps you moving forward, those precious working hours clear, and something to look forward to as a way to unwind.

4. Get complete everywhere. This will take a little longer, but also get complete on those loose ends that are hanging like strings in the wind, in other areas of your life. Take that heap of clothing to a donation box, (finally), finish the half-done home decorating or renovation project, and sort through that stack of magazines/CD's or whatever else has been piled up on a table for months. The relief you get from this will be like a weight lifted – physically and mentally.

5. Finally, (as best as you can) get emotionally complete.
If there is a relationship that needs tending to, a heart that
needs healing, or anyone that needs love or forgiveness
(yourself included), find a way to bring some completion here.
It may mean reading a book, taking a class, having a tough
conversation or getting some outside help. The completions
here can be more involved and over a longer period of time,
but the rewards are astounding.

One of my first coaches had me put a sticky note on my desk
that reads: "I do complete work." (see section 17, *Shiny Object
Syndrome*). While the sticky note comes and goes as needed,
those words continually ring out in my ears – especially when I
have a dozen browser windows and documents open. It's a
reminder to me to stop, slow down, and finish what I've
started; everything I've started. Life, after all, is not an
emergency. Do we really want to rush to get this one done?
There is great fun in beginnings! The energy is new and
moderately exciting. But completions make us nervous.
Completions mean something has ended, a new challenge is
around the corner, and it can produce mild to moderate
anxiety about "what next?"

What comes next is in part up to us – what we decide to take
on, try or begin; and partially left in the hands of fate or life
itself. There is a certain amount that's just going to happen on
its own accord anyway. The difference is, we give ourselves a
better chance of success, of moving forward and living a life of
fun, grace and ease, if we can do it on a foundation that is
strong and complete.

46. Taking Care of Your Body

"Your body always gets the final say."

- Hunter Phoenix

I'm a fairly high-energy person. I don't like to sit still much, and relaxing is something I have to work at, (wow, that sounds ridiculous!) Ridiculous as it may be, it's true. And I know I'm not alone. With life moving at a break-neck pace, many of us have high demands placed on our time and our energy. But the single truth I have learned, is that *your body always gets the final say.* You can push yourself, burn the candle at both ends, cut back on sleep and skip meals, but when your body decides it's had enough, it means it! It is no longer open to pressure tactics, threats (if you don't do this then....) or even negotiation. It will come to a full stop of its own accord. Sometimes this may be as simple as just being too tired to function and making many mistakes. It may come in the form of a migraine, cold, flu, or something much more serious. Without the co-operation of your body, the rest of your life comes to a grinding halt. Like it or not.

When our physical systems are stressed, it shows up everywhere. Looking tired and dark circles under the eyes are usually the beginning. This is also a time when your skin may break-out, or become dull and dry. Hair will often lose its luster, or fall out all together – in both men and women. Body weight may begin to fluctuate dramatically, nails break, posture droops, and these are only the exterior signs. Imagine what's going on underneath?

So how do we continue to function optimally in our fast-paced world, while still taking care of ourselves? To help you with this I've decided to share my own personal tips for staying mentally sane and physically well when dealing with the stress, pressures and the demands of a high energy life.

Nourish Your Body. This may seem obvious, but, really what are you eating? How often do you grab a fast lunch on the go that tastes only marginally better than the packaging it came in? There are always healthy alternatives, and if you commit and plan for these in advance they'll be much easier to find. A good rule of thumb: if it grows, eat it. If it doesn't, don't. If you find that a little extreme, start with baby steps. Try going one full week eating only food that doesn't come with a label.

Move Your Body. I once heard a health coach say, "If your body doesn't move, your brain thinks it's dead." I'm not sure if that's really true, but I like it! … and it stuck with me. The benefits of exercise are no secret. But even if you can't make it to gym everyday, take frequent breaks and stretch at your desk. 60 seconds, a few times a day will make a big difference. Rolling up and down through the spine is a great way to release tension and clear your head. Even turning your head side to side can help unlock tight neck and shoulder muscles that can become inflexible and painful from spending all day focused forward, towards a keyboard and a screen. Personally, I work standing up with a desk that's countertop height. I keep lots of "toys" close by; inflatable, balance disks, tennis balls, massage rollers and more, to keep my body limber and me amused :)

Soothe Your Body. Some of my favorite ways to soothe the body are massage, reflexology and soaking in a hot tub when one is available. But during the workday, essential oils and aromatherapy are my "go-to" quick fix for calming stress and tension. Lavender is especially good for bringing more balance and ease, and rosemary and peppermint are great pick-me-ups to revitalize and promote clear thinking, or even relieve a mild headache. Essential oils can be mixed and applied on the skin for personal use, or in a diffuser to scent the whole room. There are dozens to choose from, so be sure to experiment and find ones that are right for you. Visiting an aromatherapy shop or practitioner is a wonderful way to start.

Boost Your Body. Our bodies, especially when under stress need all of the physical support they can get. We need sound nutrition as building blocks, but high-performance or high stress requires some premium fuel. There are a wide variety of supplements on the market and many are formulated to fit a very specific age, gender and need. If you feel like you could use a little boost, check with a doctor, nutritionist or naturopath for a recommendation.

One of my other energy boosting secrets are morning smoothies or "power shakes". Loaded with fresh fruit, high fiber, cleansing greens and protein, these keep me energized throughout the day. An added bonus – I find myself far less hungry during the day when I start my morning with one of these. If you'd like my own personal Power Smoothie Recipe, I've included it at the back of this book.

Relax Your Body. Relaxation: simple, easy, free, and feels wonderful. Then why do we resist it so much? Most of us run around frantic all day, rushing from one task and appointment to another, only to collapse in exhaustion, (maybe in front of the TV) at day's end. Consciously giving yourself time and space to unwind, free from noise and interruption feels very different to simply collapsing and zoning out. Guided meditations are one of my favorite ways to do this – anything from 5-20 minutes with your earbuds in and eyes closed can be enormously de-stressing. If you're not the meditation type, or would just like something quicker even closing your eyes for 60 seconds throughout the day can give your brain a much needed break – especially if you spend any length of time on the computer. This can even be done easily at your desk simply by placing your head in your hands with eyes covered – it's almost like "rebooting your brain."

The tips I've shared above are from my own personal routine, but as always, be sure to check with a qualified healthcare practitioner before embarking on any new additions or changes to your diet, exercise or supplement plan.
There are hundreds of small ways we can take care of our physical being, and all have an almost instant payoff. Take care of your body. Be kind to it; it does so much for you. And really, this life is nothing without it.

Part VII
Maintaining & Enjoying

47. Just Three Things

"It's not a big thing, but I guess it's true–big things are often just small things that are noticed."
- Markus Zusak

Just this week, my mentor and coach decided to test me a little and put me on the spot. He asked me: "If you had to give three pieces of advice to a complete stranger that you felt certain would massively impact their happiness, success, and well-being, what would they be?"

For just a moment, I squirmed uncomfortably, hoping that what I would say would be profound and life changing. Then, with a wave of surrender, I decided to trust myself, and gave in to whatever came out. I realized that my advice might not be perfect for everyone, at any given moment, but it would be from the heart, and what I truly felt was important at that particular time. It also wouldn't be all encompassing – another initial worry; but it wasn't meant to be, rather just a starting point, maybe a turning point, in a brief moment in time.

Below you'll find my answers, but before you read them, I'd encourage you to take a minute or two and just come up with your own: *"If you had to give three pieces of advice to a complete stranger that you felt certain would massively impact their happiness, success, and well-being, what would they be?"* Take the time to write the answers out. Do this quickly if you can, (in just 3 or 4 minutes) trusting the first three things that come to your mind. Try to get things out before "reason" has time to take over and convince you that something else is more witty, profound or important. I've done this with a few people and received answers that are open, heartfelt and deeply revealing. It may be what we need to hear, or what we wish we had been told.

Get out a piece of paper, and write your own answers out before continuing...
1.
2.
3.
Once you've written your answers out, consider sharing these words of wisdom with those close to you, the people who matter most. Maybe this is the advice you'd like to give a friend in need, or your children, (grown or small). Or are these words that you need to hear, and act on, yourself?
If you'd like to share your wisdom with me, I'd love to hear from you.

Here is what I wrote...
1. Take care of your physical health and your body; without this, everything else becomes secondary.
2. Grow, grow, grow. Everything on this planet is either growing or dying, don't believe me, look at plants.
3. Follow what brings you joy. If money brings you joy, go for it. If playing in the park with your kids brings you joy, do more of that. When you look back on your life, are you going to wish you had done more of "what you should have" or what truly brought you joy.

See if you can take three little pieces of advice this week, even if they are your own.

48. Something To Look Forward To

"Tomorrow is the most important thing in life. Comes into us at midnight very clean. It's perfect when it arrives and it puts itself in our hands. It hopes we've learned something from yesterday."
- John Wayne

What were you looking forward to today when you got up? What about yesterday? And the day before? For most of us, our days are a long laundry list of "To Do's", "Should" and running errands, not to mention showing up for work, taking care of the kids and the list goes on.

As I continually coach clients to be more focused, organized, and more productive, I've found time and time again, that without something fun, wonderful or delicious to look forward to, simply trying to be more productive is just an added pressure and another thing on the list.

Great lives are created by living a series of great days! They don't magically happen after we've spent years running ourselves into the ground to achieve personal and professional goals. So what do you have to look forward to? This week? This Month? Later this year?

As an experiment, for the next week, see if you could find at least one thing every day to look forward to. It doesn't have to be big and flashy, just something that interests, excites or inspires you; something that would be a small indulgence.

When I asked one client to do this, he got particularly creative. With his iphone, he snapped a picture of a huge brandy snifter that now sits on his desk. It's filled with small pieces of paper with ideas on them of things he looks forward to. When he needs a boost he pulls a piece of paper from the snifter and does whatever is on it. As I think golf may have made it in there a disproportionate number of times, there are also a number non-seasonal fallbacks and smaller, quicker items ;)

For me personally, some of my "daily treats" in the last week have been a luxurious day at the beach, having lunch with a good friend, working from home on my sunny patio for few days, in summery clothes, without the bother of make-up! And taking something off of my schedule that was just getting too cumbersome to handle.

Decide the night before what "tomorrow's treat" will be, and if it's weather dependent, have a back-up. This not only gives you something fun to look forward to, but planning your indulgences will actually make you less likely to binge on your diet, or shrug off items on that always long "to do" list. Be creative, enjoy and give yourself something to look forward to!

49. Complaint Free

*"You cannot have a happy ending
to an unhappy journey."*
- **Abraham-Hicks**

How many times a day, a week a month does someone complain to you about something? Maybe it's a co-worker who seems to be in a perpetual bad mood, your kids who are never happy with what's for dinner, or a parent or spouse that constantly uses you as a sounding board. How much would you love it, if that all just stopped! And notice how merely the thought of that changes your mood, and lightens your soul.
As with many things in life, complaining is an inside job. Like it or not, it generally starts with us. We also complain to our co-workers, kids and spouses, and most of all to ourselves. How many times have you rerun the story in your head of the ex who did you wrong, the person who cut you off in traffic or the sales clerk who was so rude to you? This constant negative chatter is worse than someone else complaining – we end up nagging ourselves.

So for one week can you simply let it go? For one week, make your life a "Complaint Free Zone". A trick I use to remind myself of this is to wear a red rubber band around my wrist. Every time I catch myself complaining, I snap the band and move it to the other wrist.
Watch yourself if you have the urge to complain about traffic, the weather or politics. If you can change the situation do, and if you can't why complain about it?

For one week don't let people complain to you. Let your kids know that this week the house is Complaint Free. If they have a problem, help them solve it, but no complaining.

Living Complaint Free can lift your spirit and lighten your soul. This week have fun, stop complaining, and enjoy your week! For more ideas on living Complaint Free visit **www.AComplaintFreeWorld.org** .

50. Celebrate Your Life

"Belief in oneself is one of the most important bricks in building any successful venture."
- **Lydia M. Child**

Coaching, and any kind of growth or self-development is in part finding solutions to problems. We spend a lot of time looking at what's wrong, what isn't working, what we'd still like to do, be or accomplish. But the other part of that process is taking a moment to rejoice in our achievements and celebrate our victories and our wins - no matter how big or small.
It is fuel for the spirit and food for the soul. It keeps the work worthwhile. But when was the last time you celebrated all that you've done? All that you are? And how far you've come in this journey.

Levi Strauss used to insist that his executive employees keep a success journal on their desks. They were to record all accomplishments and achievements, big or small. Strauss was a very smart and successful man; he knew that success breeds success and greater confidence to move forward.

We've come a long way at this point in our journey, and I'd encourage you to take some time to acknowledge your success and celebrate your life. Take a few moments this week to write down all of your accomplishments – from this week, this month or this year. Notice what goals you may have achieved? How far you have come? Which things were "on your list", and what other great things you have done this year, that maybe you didn't plan?

Our successes in life are our building blocks. Each one enables us to move ahead just a little bit further, to reach a little higher and dream a little bigger! You may want to take a note from Mr. Strauss and start your own success journal, (I keep one on my desk). It not only boosts your confidence and morale on those down days, but now you have a written record of every single step you took to achieving your last big goal.

If you'd like to share your successes, feel free to contact me or visit my Facebook page (see back of book for Connecting information) I'd be honored to share in your stories.

51. Thank You!

"We have a duty to encourage one another. Many a time a word of praise or thanks or appreciation or cheer has kept a man on his feet. Blessed is the man who speaks such a word."
William Barclay

How did you feel when you read the words Thank You at the top of the page? How often does someone thank, You? And you others?

Much has been written in the last few years about the amazing influence of gratitude in our daily lives. First and foremost, there is the work of Dr. Masaru Emoto **www.Masaru-Emoto.net ,** who discovered that crystals that form in frozen water, change when specific, concentrated thoughts, are directed towards the unfrozen water. Ugly thoughts produced ugly crystals, but the most beautiful and complex are formed by "Love and Gratitude". With the human body being more than 70% water, this creates some interesting ideas.

Then there is the Go Gratitude Experiment, a 42 day online journey, designed to forever change your life through the power of gratitude. The "(k)new views" begin with the Master Key Flash Movie, about a minute and a half long and available at: **www.GoGratitude.com/Masterkey** .

We also have Wes Hopper's "Daily Gratitude" **www.DailyGratitude.com** where you can find a free e-book on the subject and more.

So what's all the rage about gratitude? Go back to the first question that I asked today; "How did you feel when you read the words Thank You?" Thank you feels good. As a matter of fact it feels great! Thank You changes the way we interact with people and the way they interact with us. So my challenge for you this time is short and sweet: it is simply for you to be more thankful. At least once a day, make a point to thank someone that you may usually fail to appreciate. At least once a day, make a point to be thankful for something that you normally take for granted. And at least once a day, find a reason to express some love and gratitude towards yourself.

Today I'm thankful for each and every one of you who has taken the time out of your life to read this book. I'm thankful for all of the clients and friends who sparked this work; your individual uniqueness delights and inspires me to learn and to grow. Today I'm thankful for my life nestled between the ocean and mountains; what a rare treat on this planet where many glimpse neither. And the tough one, today I appreciate myself for my commitment to continually change, when my mind may be willing, but my heart is screaming "no!"
Thank you's are magical, inexpensive to give, easy to use and ultimately priceless. Thank you for being you!

52. Moving Forward, Heading Back

"There is nothing I find more exciting than picking a question that I don't know the answer to and embarking on a quest for answers. It's deeply satisfying to climb into a boat like Lewis and Clark, and head west saying, "We don't know what we'll find when we get there, but we'll be sure to let you know when we get back."
- Jim Collins, from "Good To Great"

Late in 2009 I decided to take a break. One of the first things to go (unintentionally) was my newsletter and weekly coaching tips to my clients. The emails that poured in as a result were heart-warming. Many were curious and concerned; what had happened? Was I okay? Why did I stop writing? It seemed like I had just dropped off the face of the earth? Not quite. But almost.... or at least if felt like it! I'll keep the explanation short and the lesson long.

I'm a coach. Daily, weekly, monthly I encourage people, direct them, guide and inspire them to live passionate, fulfilling lit-up lives. I coax out a little extra bravery and honesty in my clients, and demand it from myself. If I'm not living my best life, how can I ask anyone else to? Late in the summer of that year, while working with a coaching exercise that I frequently use with clients, I found some holes in my own life; areas that were keeping me unhappy, stuck and dragging me down.

I got clear on a couple of dreams that I was denying in a misguided effort to stay small and safe. But we can no more stop our own growth than a tree can stop its own. Placed in the right environment with the right nutrients/support, we are all destined to reach our own special height.

Quaking in my boots, but armed with resolve and courage, I sold my house, furniture and car, put everything else in storage, and with a mere three suitcases (okay, five including carry-ons - but this was quickly whittled down to two!) I hit the road and headed south.

Again, I'm a coach. I meticulously plan, pay great attention to detail, continually push my limits and generally live an orderly, organized full rich life. So what happened? Life, unplanned and lived-out-loud suddenly got in the way.

What started out as a simple move and trip south soon led me down a path that was populated with unforeseen bumps, road blocks, visitors and fellow travelers. It included a brush with swine flu, way too many tarantulas, a couple of hand guns under the pillow, lost luggage, numerous days without reliable phone or internet, loads of lizards, little hot water, a few photographs, exhaustion and yes, even some fun.

Like Lewis and Clark, I climbed in that boat, not knowing what I'd find. But thanks to the internet - and I learned to be ever so grateful for internet; I was able to share my adventures with my tribe along the way - moving forward, still exploring; but all the while surely heading back. Back to my truest desires. Back to the distilled essence of my soul. And back to the dreams that I had shoved aside and everything that made my spirit soar!

Somewhere along the road in my travels, I re-awoke and remembered who I truly am. It brought me back to the truest, most uncluttered version of Me.

That year took me to more than a dozen cities, 6 countries and 3 continents. The lessons, adventures and friendships that came out of it, are ones that I will treasure the rest of my life. Much of this book was born in that time, a series of coaching processes to unearth hidden fears, rekindle forgotten dreams and to plan and prepare for a more incredible life ahead.

As we wind down this volume, I'd encourage you to think about your own great adventure. What would it be for you? What project or dream would you love to set sail on? What would you be willing to explore, without any idea of what you might find at the other end? What could you try, unsure of the outcome? And, what has been holding you back?
We never really know what we're going to find in life, or what's going to find us. Every day, each one of us is like Lewis & Clark, setting out on a journey and reporting back upon our return. But the key is to do it with an open heart and open mind, for that's when the greatest discoveries and miracles can occur.
As you ponder those questions, I hope you make some wonderful discoveries of your own; discoveries that will propel you forward with your life while heading back to what's most important.
Until next time… From My Heart to Yours, Hunter

"Now and then it's good to pause in our pursuit of happiness and just be happy."

- Guillaume Apollinaire
19th century French poet

Fabulous Free Bonuses & Downloads

Success doesn't come just from reading a book; we have to take the time to implement what we've learned. To help you with this I've created some great **templates and worksheets,** and they are yours absolutely free!

All you have to do to get your totally FREE Downloads and Coaching Worksheets is visit

www.PerfectLivesBook.com/bonuses

You'll find all of the instructions there.

What Do You Get?

- Best Year of Your Life Plan

- Monthly Planner Worksheet

- New Daily Habits Action Sheet

- Energy Drains Checklist

- Values Test

- Positive Affirmations

All as a special thank you for allowing me into your life by buying and reading this book. Enjoy!

My Morning "Greens" / Power Smoothie

As promised, here is my yummy recipe for "Morning Greens". And before you turn up your nose and run away with visions of lawn clippings in a glass, please know that "I don't do unpleasant". One small sip of this blended beverage and you'll be hooked! Time and again friends have asked for my secret recipe, so here it is.

Combine the following ingredients in a blender:
One ripe banana
Additional fruit, depending on what you have fresh – a few strawberries, slices of apple, melon, mango, papaya, etc. (stay away from grapes - the skin makes a bitter-ish drink!)
One scoop of protein powder (low carb to high protein ratio)
* Approximately one tablespoon of each: bran and wheat germ
* Approximately one teaspoon of each: sunflower seeds, hemp seeds and flax seeds
(*these dry ingredients I mix together in large batches and scoop some out daily)
Two teaspoons of greens power – Phytoberry, Udo's Choice and Greens Force are my favorites for taste and nutritional content
One tablespoon of liquid chlorophyll (wonderful for cleaning the blood!)
One tablespoon of liquid silica (amazing for skin, hair and nails!)
4 ounces of your favorite fruit juice
4 ounces of filtered water
Optional: some sliced fresh ginger root and one small vial of Ginseng drink

Now blend until smooth and frothy, and enjoy!
This drink absolutely keeps me going. Without it, I'm tired, hungry and low energy throughout the day.
Smiles, Hunter

About The Author

Hunter Phoenix is a Certified Life & Success Coach & Mentor, national speaker and the creator of the Life By Design™ & Biz Breakthrough™ Coaching Systems. She helps clients strike the sweet spot between simple self-care and accelerated growth, designing their lives and businesses rather than living them by default. Hunter has worked with men and women in the entertainment industry, the legal profession, health care industries, artists, executives, business owners and entrepreneurs across North America.

Hunter is regularly called on by the media to comment on a range of issues related to personal growth and success, always with an eye on life balance and well-being.

You can find out more about Hunter at:

www.HunterPhoenixCoaching.com

Connecting...

Let's connect. This is MORE than just a book, it's a comprehensive multi-dimensional coaching program. And I'm here to help You create a life and business you LOVE.

How do we do that? Getting connected. Staying connected. And playing full on in this game.

Everything about this book (or close to it!) is at:

www.PerfectLivesBook.com Sign-up for the latest updates, releases, speaking, and book signings. I'd love to connect with you in person :)

Cool Free Downloads:

www.PerfectLivesBook.com/bonuses These are a must. Carefully chosen to produce BIG results, these are actual coaching exercises that I use with my private clients.

Download + Do = Grow *(which means more of getting what you want)*

Ask a Question, Get an Answer. Weekly hot tips and cool deals. Jump in the conversation. I love connecting at

www.HunterPhoenix.com/Facebook

Tweet about it, or get in direct conversation with me on Twitter: **@Hunter_Phoenix**

Twitter hashtag for Perfect Lives and Other Fairy Tales:

#LifeBK

Download **My Perfect Life Tour Guide**. A free guide for creating a group coaching experience or starting a book club.

HunterPhoenixCoaching.com is the full experience where

you can access...

Weekly Coaching Tips on the blog

Video & Audio Coaching Minutes

Sign-up for weekly "Power Bytes"

And lots of other cool useful resources… growing all the time.

Connect with an online community

Get one-on-one personal attention from me when you're ready to take the Next Big Leap.

Did you love this book? Find it useful, helpful, motivating or inspiring? If yes, we'd love to hear from you! Visit www.Amazon.com to review and tell the world.
Recommend it to a friend, or simply have your voice heard.

Made in the USA
Charleston, SC
25 November 2013